IT'S NOT A COW

Phil Bass

ISBN 979-8-88644-849-8 (Paperback)
ISBN 979-8-88644-851-1 (Hardcover)
ISBN 979-8-88644-850-4 (Digital)

Covenant Books
11661 Hwy 707
Murrells Inlet, SC 29576
www.covenantbooks.com

This book is dedicated to all the hardworking farmers and ranchers helping to feed the world and my favorite rancher of all, Tina.

CONTENTS

PREFACE

Hi, I'm Phil Bass. I'm three-quarters Italian by ancestry. No, Bass is not Italian. From my best estimate, it's English/Irish/Scottish-ish. But that's based off of some rather extensive lineage investigation by my late grandfather. The rest is very Italian. I grew up being reminded of that almost daily, and to be honest, I'm quite grateful for that. I'm telling you all this because I believe my youth was a remnant of the old-world Italian immigrant families who very much valued food and where it comes from.

Often, I recall discussing at the breakfast table what we will be eating for dinner. It was normal…to me. It still is. My *nonni* 's (loosely, *grandmothers* in Italian) would often compliment my cousins and me on "what good eaters we are." It's a bit of a badge of honor in families of Italian heritage. It probably goes back to times when our grandparents and their immediate families (think 1920s European immigrants) had to go without. It's probably why we value food so much.

I love food. It's a universal language. It's a bridge between cultures. Meat and milk, although not accepted by all cultures, are definitely two that have been part of mine, and have helped me share and make connections with others throughout the years. Beef and dairy products have been a part of my family culture for quite some time. My family, as well as my wife's (she's from Swiss stock), has raised beef cattle for as long as I can remember and from my understanding, nearly since my Italian ancestors set foot in North America around a hundred years ago. They have also, in some form or fashion, been a part of the dairy business for just as long. The partnership that our family has had with animals, especially cattle, is immense, and it's fun to share that with many others across the country and around the world.

My family taught me about milking cows and harvesting cattle for meat from a very tender age. Dad likes to tell the story about when my *nonno* (*grandfather* in Italian) came to borrow a meat saw from my dad because he was going to butcher a steer. He says I was crying and running after my *nonno's* truck because he didn't invite me to help him butcher the steer. Apparently, I was upset. In fact, to this day, I'd still be bummed if my family did a little meat cutting without inviting me.

Meat, and the processing thereof, has not only been nourishment but also a pastime. My earliest memories connect back to the smell of the sausage that my family makes, which, I have learned, is rather unique. Meat and milk, and where they come from, are part of my life. I'm so fortunate to have had the ability to see calves born. I'm so blessed to know where my steak comes from and how to cut it myself. I'm grateful for the fact that it's all so normal and part of everyday life for me. I know it's not the same for everyone.

It's time to tell that story. There are many folks who do not have these connections, who do not have the understanding of where their food comes from—by no fault of their own, mind you—who do not have the precious cultural connection to food and may see it only as sustenance and not part of the richness of life. I want to help tell that narrative.

I'm not a grain farmer. I'm not a vegetable farmer (that's more my wife's expertise). I'm a meatcutter and a part-time cattle rancher. I love cutting meat and making delightful delicacies from it. I love to see faces light up when they taste some sausage or salami that I and my family have made. I love watching our cattle graze and later on chew their cud contently. Meat is so nourishing, satiating, and delightful. The animals that we harvest meat from are amazing, and they have a noble purpose: to help sustain our lives.

I want to share that excitement and delight with the world. I realize that not everyone will agree with what is said in this book. In fact, I'm sure that I'll receive some criticism by many folks for many reasons. That's okay. However, this is the true story of cattle farming and ranching, and it's time it was told in a more lengthy narrative for those who may not have direct ties to agriculture. This is to simply tell the story of animal agriculture, of my family who still engages in such pursuits, of my coworkers and colleagues in animal science, and of all of those farmers and ranchers who rely on cattle to feed their families, pay their bills, and maintain their way of life, who have not the voice or the means to share what is truly an amazing story of meat-and-milk food production for humanity.

I love talking about cattle. It's why I've finally decided to write down a bit of the story that I have been telling for decades so that more people can find some of the passion I have for this amazing creature. Furthermore, the story of cattle cannot be told in a so-called "elevator speech" or in a thirty-second sound bite. The cattle story is far greater and deeper than a small snapshot and deserves to be given more time than that to be shared. Hopefully, once you, the reader, reach the last page, you'll have a new appreciation for cattle and why I hold them and the people who care for them in such high regard. Beyond their gorgeous eyes, their earthy smell, and their tasty foods that they ultimately produce, cattle are a way of life, and I couldn't imagine the world without them.

INTRODUCTION

In the United States, it is estimated that only around one percent of the population is directly involved in agriculture—all of agriculture. That means that those of us who live in the world of food and fiber production for the consuming world (that's the whole thing, by the way) have a lofty job to continue to provide the service of growing the products and byproducts that keep us fed, clothed, and living in a convenient and polite society. What I have found, however, is that in my crusade for teaching the rest of the population about agriculture, especially animal agriculture, not only has it become an uphill battle to share the good news of modern food production but that the farming and ranching population have almost been labeled as greedy capitalists bent on inhumane treatment of animals and laying waste to the environment in which farming and ranching are conducted. This couldn't be further from the truth.

The farming and ranching community, especially in the United States, is more tied to the land and natural resources than the remainder of the population could ever dream. It is the land and environment that not only allow for the growth of the food, animals, and products, but it is also the home of those who do the farming and ranching. Therefore, it would not make any more sense for a farmer or rancher to harm their home any more than a barbershop owner to set fire to their shop at the end of the day. The farming and ranching community value the land, natural resources, and environment greatly and have long been the caretakers of those entities since time eternal. However, because of the disparity between those who live in that world and those who do not, there are obvious differences in understanding that have arisen.

This book is an attempt to reach out to the world and show a small snapshot of a part of agriculture in which I spend most of my life, the cattle community. This is not meant to be a scientific text, nor is it meant to be all-encompassing. However, the goal is to use general terms that most folks can understand and relate to in an effort to explain an extremely complex and highly vibrant system of food production that has been a part of this country long before it ever was a country.

I do hope that a few of my colleagues in the animal sciences have a chance to peruse this bit of reading, but it is not designed for that audience; they already know the story. It is for those who might be curious about how a rib eye steak goes from the gleam in a young bull's eye to a celebratory dinner out with friends. It is meant to share the amazing efforts by the ranching community to help maintain the balance of natural resources that this amazing country has to offer while allowing for the love and passion of life with cattle that my family has known for generations (and I hope generations to come).

The title of the book is inspired by the misnomer that most folks use to describe a domesticated bovine animal, cattle, which most call a *cow*. We'll dive into why that might not be the most appropriate terminology, but far more than merely splitting hairs over the word used to describe non-gender-specific cattle, I plan to dive far deeper into what makes these animals so amazing and to hopefully help everyone come to appreciate the incredible animal that are cattle.

I'm sure I'll miss some specific details here and there, which means I hope I receive letters (more likely, e-mail) from those reading this to further enhance the dialogue about the mysterious animal that inspires many to live the cowboy life.

CHAPTER 1

It's Not a Cow—Well, Sometimes It Is

First things first, let's cover some terminologies. I recall at a very early age my parents gently correcting me when I called every animal that had four legs and made a *mooing* sound a cow. My confusion was further exacerbated when I would watch the public television shows in the mornings that were meant to teach kids vocabulary, and all of those mooing creatures were once again called cows—still incorrect. And finally, my young mind was blown when I learned that all my cowboy heroes growing up were neither boys, nor rarely were they ever roping and driving *cows*. Now those in the agriculture community will quickly realize to what it is I am referring and are probably having a little bit of a smirk appear on the corner of your mouth. However, for the remaining ninety-nine percent of the readership, what I'm referring to is that not all *cows* are cows.

Let's get a little scientific for a second. To be precise by an animal husbandry specialists account, a cow is a sexually mature female bovine who has had at least one calf. Usually, this occurs around year two in the life of most female cat-tle. They are the ones carrying on the lineage of the noble beast and should certainly be commended for their efforts of their nine-month gestation (yes, cattle pregnancy is about the same as in humans). However, I'm not so sure that such a contribution to the species deserves all of said species to receive the title *cow*. Indeed, cows make up a very large part of the total population of cattle. However, there are certainly a few other players in the game that deserve some credit.

The counterpart to the mature female that we now know as a cow is the *bull*. Probably not a surprise to most folks that the males are called bulls, but far too many times in my life have I heard someone describe male cattle as "bull cows" (sigh). Bulls are not as prevalent as cows in the population of the beef cattle herd. Yes, biology dictates that half of the babies (calves in this case) are going to be male and half female. It is what happens to those bulls early on in life that commands whether or not they receive a new moniker, but let's hold on to that thought for a moment.

A common observation from my years of introducing the general public to livestock is the thought that "the bulls have horns and the cows don't." This is an unfortunate misunderstanding. It's not the gender of the animal that decides whether or not they have horns (they're not deer, which, in that case, is referring to antlers) but rather the genetic makeup. Some breeds of cattle grow horns, some do not. More to come on that front.

Bulls and cows in the cattle world can also have yet another term associated to them when they become parents. If you hear a rancher ever say the word *dam*, there are certainly a few things to which they may be referring (English is a funny language). In one circumstance, if one has stubbed their toe, received an unexpected bill in the mail, or watched their dog tear off after a varmint and soon their barking becomes a faint yip as they drift off into the abyss of forest foliage, you may indeed hear a rancher say something that sounds like *dam*. Of course, the precise term to which they are referring is the expletive that ends in an N, but let's not dwell on that for now.

Alternatively, you may hear a rancher use the word *dam* if they are indeed water management experts during the monsoon season or in the presence of a beaver. But that's not connected to the cattle term.

A *dam* in the cattle world, both beef and dairy, is used to describe the mother cow in a bovine relationship that has produced an offspring. Surprisingly, according to the dictionary with which I have recently referenced, the word *dam* is derived from Middle English and is similar to the term *dame*, which is in reference to a mother or lady. Who knew cattle were so proper (proceed to raise pinky elegantly in the air)? Well, let's not stop there with the fancy terms then. It turns out that the male parent, the bull, is actually known as a *sire*. Did you think that you would read a book about cattle and learn that the cattle parents are referred to in near-royal terms? Fascinating!

Well, that's enough about talking about the parents, let's dig into what we call the younger herd members. Many folks probably are familiar with what baby cattle are called, but let's define it, nonetheless. Baby cattle are called calves. In fact, when a cow is giving birth, that process is actually called *calving*. As I've mentioned, calves take about nine months to be made before they're ready to join the farmyard populace.

Most beef calves are born weighing between eighty to 110 pounds and are able to stand and nurse within a couple of hours of life. This is important because of the need for calves to receive a special kind of milk from their mothers called colostrum. Colostrum is an energy-dense milk packed with antibodies that the new mother makes for only a short period of time. That's okay because the digestive tract of the newborn calf can only absorb the antibodies in that milk for a very short period of time anyway.

Both the mother's colostrum production and the calf's colostrum-absorption ability last about twenty-four hours after birth. Soon after that twenty-four-hour window, the mother's mammary gland transitions to making the white milk that most folks would recognize as something similar to what would be put on your cereal in the morning. Colostrum, however, looks more like eggnog, slightly yellow and thick. Those who have worked around livestock know just how critical it is to get those newborn animals to nurse as those antibodies, passed to the calf from the cow via the colostrum, are necessary for preventing the calves from catching a disease—that is, until they are able to build up their own immunities.

Beef calves live with their mothers generally for about six to seven months, solely nursing early on but quickly learning the trade that they are best known for: grazing. Calves need a slow transition to solid foods, somewhat like people. However, unlike people, cattle can eat grass and can thrive on it, but we'll discuss that later. During the time next to their mothers, they will often receive some special treatment to be sure that they are healthy and accounted for. Oftentimes, calves will receive something called an ear tag. Imagine a large plastic earring, which can come in a variety of shapes, colors, and forms, but the purpose is to be able to identify them from their herd mates. In the case of some cattle breeds—for example, the Angus breed, which in most cases is solid black—the calves may all look the same at first glance, so ranchers use ear tags in many cases to identify the individuals and be able to keep records on them such as birth weight, growth rate, sex, parentage, etc.

In many states in the Western US the use of brands is still a prevalent form of identification. Branding requires the heating of a steel iron to near red-hot and creating a permanent brand mark on the animal to denote ownership of the cattle. This is often done when the calves are young, and they seem to recover quite quickly as a result. Branding is a fantastic identifier and lasts much longer and is more effective in some cases than an ear tag that may fade or fall out. However, hot branding, as it is known, does receive some negative press as it does cause a bit of pain to the animal. Many farmers and ranchers who hot brand now are considering using some form of pain reliever to help the calf recover quicker from the obligatory event. Hot brands are permanent identifiers but are not usually used for individual animal identification. That's where ear tags come in.

Another thing that may happen to beef calves when they are rather young is that some of the bull calves (look at us using animal terminology) that are destined for meat production undergo castration. For those who are not accustomed to animal agriculture, this may seem like a rather intense measure and don't see the need to subject a calf to such a treatment. However, those who do live and work with livestock regularly know just how important a step this is in maintaining the safety of both other animals and people around them, and it helps improve meat quality later on for the males of the species, but that's later on as well.

Let's think about this: full-grown bulls have been considered for a long time, in many cultures, as a form of powerful masculinity. And, well, it's true. Mature bulls can be aggressive and at times dangerous to be around, and for many ranchers who do work with bulls regularly, they know that mature bulls have a tendency to break things. To better manage the bull calves later on in life, many are castrated. Castrating a bull calf will produce what is then called in the cattle community a *steer*. This process of castrating livestock is far from a new idea and has been used for hundreds, if not thousands, of years in many cultures and in many different species (horses, geldings; pigs, barrows; chickens, capons; sheep, wethers; etc.). The process is rather quick and simple, and in most cases, it is done surgically when the calf is very young.

There are processes that are considered more *humane* by using a rubber band around the cord leading to the testicles of the bull calf, but what animal behavior specialists have seen is that the surgical-castration method using a sharp instrument, like a knife or scalpel, tends to cause the least amount of mental and physical trauma to the calf, and they recover quite quickly. It may be a process that's a little hard for those outside the agriculture community to swallow but a very common practice that is necessary and done in a quick and systematic approach to minimize the impact on the animal so that it can get back to doing what cattle do.

Aside from a steer, which is usually going to be castrated cattle of a younger age (about two years or less), their gender counterpart would be what is known as a *heifer*. A heifer is a term used for young female cattle that have yet to have a calf. This can be a term used to describe a brand-new baby female calf all the way up until she has reached maturity and is about to give birth for the first time. Now, just to make things a bit more curious, we in the cattle community will often call a heifer that has just had her first calf as a "first-calf heifer" even though she could technically be called a cow now. These are our newest of cattle mothers and are often given that unique descriptor because they also regularly require a bit more attention from the farmer or rancher who is charged with caring for her and her offspring. Just like a new human mother may need a little extra coaching and help from friends and family, a first-calf heifer may need just a little extra help that first time around. However, once she's ready to have her next calf, she's usually a pro by then and can handle herself just fine with minimal assistance from the rancher.

As you can see, the cattle community has a lot of unique terminology. In this instance, we have only discussed the basics of what to call the animal in its different forms. As we progress through this book, we'll cover more terms to broaden your knowledge of cattle vocabulary.

CHAPTER 2

It's Not a Cow—It's a Rainbow!

Although cattle don't literally come in every color of the rainbow, there's no question that they do have a colorful background and lineage. Cattle also have far more external appearances than the stereotypical common black-and-white of the predominant dairy cattle breed (which is known as a Holstein, by the way) depicted in so many cartoons and images. There's a lot more to cattle than what first meets the eye.

Domesticated cattle, as we know them today, come from the ancient species known as *Bos primigenius*, also known as the *aurochs* cattle. Aurochs cattle were famously depicted in the prehistoric cave paintings in Chauvet and Lascaux in France more than fifteen thousand years ago. Aurochs cattle are now extinct (last one died in Poland in the 1600s), but there are a few breeds around that are similar to that once-dominant species.

The current species of cattle are the *Bos taurus* and *Bos indicus* cattle. In general, *Bos taurus* cattle are those native to Europe, whereas *Bos indicus* are more native to Africa and the subcontinent of India.

Bos taurus

As mentioned, the *Bos taurus* species of cattle are those that would be most familiar with those found in most of North America and Europe. These cattle are often large framed and muscular (with the exception of the popular dairy breeds) and are often well adapted to cooler northern climates. Common breeds of *Bos taurus* include the following:

- *Angus.* Natives to Scotland, Angus cattle are a breed focused on beef production and have been for many generations. Angus cattle are either solid black or red in color. However, in the United States, the Angus breed is black whereas the separate Red Angus breed are the red ones. Angus cattle are polled, which means they naturally never grow horns.
- *Hereford.* A breed of cattle native to England, the Hereford were once by far the most popular breed of beef cattle in North America during the early to mid-1900s prior to the current dominance of Angus. Hereford come both horned and polled and have a distinctive red body coloring with a white face. Crossbreeding with Hereford and Angus is common and result in an animal with a black body

but a white face and are called a "black baldy" in the business.

- *Charolais.* Big with a solid-white hair coat, the Charolais (pronounced shar-lay) cattle are originally from France. Charolais were once used for draft (pulling farm implements and wagons), which helped them grow into the mighty animal they are today. Although not as popular as Angus and Hereford for beef production, Charolais have certainly made their mark in the US beef herd.
- *Simmental.* A native of Switzerland, the Simmental breed has changed a lot over the years. In the modern beef herd, Simmental cattle will be either solid black or red, but they were originally a brown-and-white color, which can still be seen in parts of Europe. Years of selective breeding and cross-breeding has led the Simmental breed to resemble Angus cattle. Simmental are rapid-growing beef cattle and a popular breed in the United States.
- *Holstein, Jersey, Guernsey, Brown Swiss, and Ayrshire (oh my).* The dominant dairy breeds. We'll visit these later.

Cattle that fall under the *Bos taurus* grouping are going to be the most commonly found beef cattle breeds in the United States. These can be subdivided into two additional categories: British and continental. As the name implies, the British breeds are ones native to the British Isles, whereas the continental breeds are those that were developed over the years on the mainland of Europe. Although many a Scottish denizen would take offense to calling the Angus a British breed, the fact is that they still fall under that category along with the Hereford cattle. Continental cattle would include the Charolais and Simmental, among many other breeds.

Historically, continental cattle were larger in frame than that of the British breeds, which has lent well to cross-breeding over the years to increase size and growth potential of beef calves. Although they adapt well to most environments, there are certainly other breeds of cattle that have a tendency to perform better in warmer climates.

Bos indicus

Most commonly found in the Southeastern US, the *Bos indicus* species of cattle are very distinctive in shape and appearance. Now I'm not saying that they have five legs and Pegasus-like wings, but it doesn't take a trained animal scientist to pick out an animal with *Bos indicus* influence. *Bos indicus* cattle have the very obvious large neck hump crest between their shoulders, often have an elongated face, long ears, and extra skin. All of these unique features help these cattle dissipate heat in very warm, often humid environments.

Interestingly, because of the climate for which they are adapted often contains insects and parasites in relatively higher amounts than that of northern climates, these cattle have also developed a bit of a resistance to those rascally bugs. If anyone has spent time in Alabama, Mississippi, Louisiana, Georgia, or Florida, you know that what I am describing is descriptive to the environment found in those states. *Bos indicus* cattle are well adapted to that sultry environment, and as a result, you'll see them in more quantity there than in the more northern states. Breeds of *Bos indicus* cattle include the following:

- *Brahman.* The dominant breed of *Bos indicus* cattle in North America, Brahman cattle are white or silver in color. Although well adapted to hot and humid climates, their meat is not yet prized as much as the *Bos taurus* cattle and, therefore, are often crossed with British breeds of cattle in an effort to improve their carcass quality traits.
- *Nellore.* Also a predominantly white breed of *Bos indicus*, Nellore cattle are the dominant breed in the beef-producing powerhouse of the South American country of Brazil. Much of Brazil is at or around the earth 's equator, thereby needing a breed that can handle heat and humidity.
- *Brangus.* As the name implies, Brangus is a cross between Brahman and Angus cattle. They maintain the large neck hump, floppy ears, extra skin, and the warm climate hardiness while incorporating some of the meat carcass traits that make the Angus breed so popular. Their hides are almost always solid black (or red with the Red Angus type).

Wagyu

Since this tome is being written in the twenty-first century, it is only right to make sure that the breed that has become to some as the holy grail of beef be mentioned. Wagyu (quite literally meaning "black cattle" in Japanese) are a menagerie of *Bos taurus* breeds that, over many years, have been selected for marbling, marbling, and more marbling. Briefly, marbling is the little flecks of fat inside the muscle that deliver taste in a steak. These animals, although somewhat slow growing compared to traditional beef breeds, are genetically predisposed to very high amounts of marbling in their meat. Many say that meat from a well-finished prized Wagyu animal will appear as little flecks of muscle in the fat (a bit of a sarcastic description, but you get the point).

Now, just like all cattle breeds, there are high-quality Wagyu, and there are so-so Wagyu. We'll discuss further later on the different levels of quality of beef, but for now, just know that these animals are impressive when it comes to creating decadent meat—beef fat, the other *other* white meat!

CHAPTER 3

It's Not a Cow—It's a Miracle!

've shouted this phrase from the rooftops for many years. Cattle are freaking miracles! These are creatures that have the ability to take something that we as humans cannot eat (i.e., grass) and turn it into something that is both nutritious and tasty: meat and milk. How can that be? Well, it has to do with the way that cattle digestive tracts are set up. They are very different from the way that ours is designed.

We humanoids (or at least that is what I assume is the primary readership of books) have a more simplified digestive tract that is called a monogastric system. Monogastrics such as ourselves have a single stomach compartment (therefore, the prefix *mono*) that primarily is designed to break down protein while mixing other food items in preparation for digestion later on down the line. Other monogastrics would include pigs, dogs, and cats. Cattle, however, are *ruminants*, which means they have more of a four-compartment stomach system that is capable of fermentation.

Wait, what? Four stomachs? Yep, but they—the stomachs, that is—don't all do the same thing, and that's the key.

Ruminants are named after the large first compartment of their stomach system called a rumen. Think of the rumen as a very large fermentation vat used in a similar way to how one would make sauerkraut or beer. For those less familiar with the process of fermentation, let's visit that for a second. Fermentation is the biochemical breakdown of carbon-based compounds essentially into energy, often in the absence of oxygen. Fermentation is often considered a means of energy production by yeasts and bacteria, but it also technically can happen in muscles as well.

In our cases with cattle, we're looking at some very specific bacteria that do the fermentation work. These primary bacteria are able to take parts of a plant that our bodies cannot digest and use the sugars that are in that plant to create energy or at least compounds that can be used to make energy in the animal. This complicated process is a prime example of how "you are what you eat" is not always the case, and it gets even more complicated when we dig into just exactly what plants can bring to the table, so to speak.

When we think of plants and sugars, most people will think of white table sugar that is made from sugar beets, and this is certainly a source of sugar. However, when we look in the biological sciences world, we find that sugar is even a complicated topic. To be precise, we call sugars *carbohydrates*. What that means is that their chemical makeup is pretty much "carbon, hydrogen, and oxygen." Our very common carbohydrate we talk about is glucose, a molecule of six carbons, twelve hydrogens, and six oxygens. This is a very simply sugar that microbes love to use as a food source, especially during fermentation.

What's even more interesting is how these simple sugars can be built into chains of more complex sugars. The more complex sugars certainly have the same basic makeup but are now in a longer chain-type molecule. These long-chain molecules can come in two basic forms: starch and cellulose. Now I know that my friends in the nutrition world (animal and human) will now count down to eye roll initiation considering how much I'm simplifying all of this scientific information, but this isn't a college text book. It's meant to be an easy way for most folks to understand what's happing in the tummy of a cow (okay, now too simplistic). Anyway, what we're talking about are essentially two forms of the same building blocks just assembled differently in the plant in order to provide different functions to the plant.

Starch is a fantastic energy storage means in a plant and is what we talk about when we are referring to *carbs* in our (i.e., human) diet. If someone is trying to "cut out the carbs" in their diet, they are generally referring to the starches that are found in seeds, grain, and tubers (potatoes). What most folks don't realize is that the leafy green vegetables that are eaten are actually carbohydrates as well. They are just in an indigestible form for us monogastrics. This is because of a minor adjustment in the molecular makeup of the sugars where the linkages in the chain of those carbohydrates are slightly different in what we call *cellulose* compared to *starch*. However, that slight difference in how the linkages are made will mean the difference in the parts of the plants that are the tasty seed and the parts that are the structural stem and leaf. *Wow*, science is cool and subtle.

Anyway, the whole point of going down the road of explaining starches and cellulose is that ruminants can use both as energy sources (again, we cannot). The reason for this is because they have specialized bacteria and other microbes in their rumen that can break the bonds between the glucose molecules, allowing the fermentation organisms access to the simple sugars (e.g., glucose). Once the simple sugars are accessed and used by the fermentation microbes, the useful byproducts from that fermentation are things called "volatile fatty acids." What that means is that these compounds are able to easily be absorbed into the bloodstream of the animal, travel to the liver, and be rebuilt into useful sugars in the body for energy use in places like muscle and other working tissue. Excess energy is stored as fat.

During fermentation of starches, the compounds that make up the starches are more easily used up, and there are not many *leftover* compounds. However, when ruminants ferment cellulose, they can generate some leftover compounds as a result of an incomplete fermentation, so to speak. The leftovers in this case are generally hydrogen molecules (remember that carbohydrates are made up of a lot of hydrogens). These hydrogen molecules, if left to wander about in a rumen, will eventually begin to lower the pH of the rumen, making the environment very acidic.

Now if the rumen were a stomach like a monogastric's, then the acidity wouldn't be a problem, but too much acidity in a rumen can really cause problems in that compartment, so there are ancient bacteria in the rumen called *methanogens* who get to work. These specialized bacteria collect the extra hydrogen and combine them with carbon atoms to form a compound with one carbon and four hydrogens, also known as methane. This methane is now safer for the animal, but because it is a gas, it still needs to be expelled from the rumen. This process is known as eructation.[1]

There's a whole interest in more forage (grass) finished beef. Honestly, as long as there's interest in beef in general, I'm happy. However, it comes down to the reasoning. For those who like the more intense flavor of grass-finished beef, then by all means dig in! Yet there are some who believe that grass-finishing beef is better for the environment than traditional grain-finished beef. This is a little counterintuitive.

---

[1] For several years now, it has been brought to the attention of many that cow farts are adding to carbon equivalents in the atmosphere, which is believed by some to be leading to climate change. Although cattle do produce methane regularly, the amount of flatulation that cattle will produce is inconsequential to the eructation that allows the methane to be released after fermenting forages (grass). Those who are concerned with cattle methane production should actually be more concerned with the burps of cattle, not the farts. Regardless of the end of the animal from which it comes, the amount of methane actually produced by cattle fermentation is rather small compared to the atmospheric carbon equivalents of many other industrial, electricity production, and transportation means. Furthermore, the little bit of methane that is produced due to rumen fermentation is a result of these miraculous creatures eating things that we cannot eat (i.e., grass) and turning it into highly nutritious things we can eat (i.e., milk and meat). I'd say that's a very worthwhile endeavor. I'll take one less international flight if I can be able to enjoy a tasty treat from our ruminant companions.

The overwhelming majority of cattle do indeed spend most of their lives eating and foraging for grass in pasture and on rangeland, both of which, in most cases, are not suitable for farming anything else. But it's the finishing phase of the animal's life that makes the big impact on their growth as they reach market weight and begin to deposit the specific types of fat in their body that will contribute to the certain flavors that are expressed when we enjoy the meat from those animals.

Most cattle in North America are finished in feed yards, where they can have a very precisely balanced ration of forages (hay and grass), starches (grains, potatoes, or bakery byproducts), protein (soybean meal, distiller's byproducts, etc.), and supplemental vitamins and minerals to maintain their nutrition, health, and growth. This is the time when these animals will become the most efficient as far as carbohydrate fermentation is concerned. Because they will have higher amounts of starch carbohydrates in their diets, they produce less methane than an animal eating only grass/cellulose, and as a result, they will burp less methane. The starches also help the cattle deposit the really tasty buttery beef fat that we will investigate further in a later chapter. Ruminants are very dynamic creatures that can use a lot of byproducts that we would otherwise not have value for.[2]

---

[2] Byproducts of farming and food production are excellent feed resources for cattle. Soybean meal is the leftover from making soybean/vegetable oil. After the soybean is crushed and pressed for the oils in it, the byproduct left over is a protein-rich polenta-looking mash that cattle can eat for their protein source. Cattle are also a big help when it comes to using the leftovers from making ethanol—you know, the stuff that is mixed into gasoline that we put in our cars. Ethanol is produced from

A question I've been asked in the past is, "Do cattle really need grain in their diet?" Or even more precise is the question, "Aren't cattle designed to eat grass, not grain?" Well, the answer is that they are designed to eat both. There are microbes in their rumen that target grass fermentation, and there are microbes that target grain fermentation. This is because if you think of how grass grow in nature, they have both the stem (cellulose) and seed (grain/starch). If you let your lawn grow unattended, you'll see it "head out," which means it has gone to seed. This is literally what grain farmers do intentionally. Now we in the animal science community are just more aware of how to mix the feed for cattle to optimize their digestion, and we can, in a sense, provide for the microbes in the rumen exactly what they need to work most effectively.

And by the way, for those who say, "Well, what about corn?" well, corn—or maize, which is how most other countries know it as—is technically a really tall-growing grass that grows really well in the latitudes and environment of much of North America. We're just using the resources that are available depending on where the cattle are raised: corn in the central plains and Midwest, potatoes in the Pacific Northwest, barley in Canada, and so on.

---

grain (mostly corn) farming in North America. The ethanol is fermented using a similar process that is used for making whisky, just on a massive scale. The stuff that remains from the ethanol-making process looks like porridge in the wet form and corn meal in the dry form. Either way, the byproduct known as "distiller's grains" are also high in protein and fiber, both great for cattle to grow on. Interestingly, this is not a new idea as people even in colonial New England fed the leftovers from whiskey distilling and beer making to their livestock, especially cattle.

Now, I've mentioned that cattle have four compartments to their stomach system, and we've only really talked about one, the rumen. But that's because it's a big deal, both literally and figuratively. The rumen makes up about eighty percent of the *stomachs* of the ruminant animal. In a full-grown steer, the rumen can hold up to twenty-five gallons of feed or more, but there are three other compartments that ruminants have that also help with digestion.

The smallest of the ruminant animal compartments is the *reticulum*. The reticulum has a honeycomb layer inside, and it helps with the contractions of the rumen itself. The reticulum can also help sort the smaller pieces of ingested feed from the larger. Small pieces pass to the next stomach compartment, larger pieces stay in the rumen and ferment more.

The next compartment is the *omasum*. This is an area that helps absorb or recycle water in a biological sense. The water that is in the feed and rumen can help hydrate the animal. The omasum can also absorb electrolytes and some volatile fatty acids (remember, that's the product of fermentation in the rumen).

The final compartment in the ruminant is the *abomasum*. This compartment acts very similar to ours in that it is acidic and helps break down proteins for digestion. The abomasum is often referred to as the *true* stomach.

After the stomach compartments, the ruminant animal is pretty similar in makeup to us monogastrics. They absorb nutrients in their intestines and process things in a similar way to how we do. It's the magical rumen, the big fermentation vat, that makes cattle so special!

This lends the value of cattle to partner with humans in ways that go far beyond the making of meat and milk. Cattle are able to help with weed and brush control in ways that would be very hard to manage with human mechanical or chemical means. Cattle can eat grass and bushes in wildland areas that could have the potential to be fuels for forest fires. Cattle also like to rub and scratch on trees, which helps to clean up the low-lying and dead branches that could also exacerbate a forest fire situation.

Cattle also are great at aerating grasslands that have developed thatch and compaction on and in the soils. They can puncture through old grass' thatch and compacted ground and allow for better circulation of oxygen and nutrients to reach the soil, which eventually leads to healthier green spaces. Cattle can also be great at going places, such as mountains and hills, that farming equipment and wheeled transportation cannot. This means that cattle can be sent out into a forested and mountainous landscape, and they will climb and forage for grass and leaves, all the while growing either themselves or another calf that will be the next generation of cattle for food. This allows for places like the Rocky Mountains, Sierra Nevada, and the Sawtooth Mountains in the Western US to be used for food production in the form of beef, places that otherwise cannot be farmed for human food.

This also allows for places with very shallow soil depths, like the Nebraska Sandhills and the Kansas Flint Hills, to also be able to produce food in the form of beef that otherwise would not be able to be farmed as tilling the soil in those places would have devastating environmental consequences. Cattle can be great land stewards during their adolescent phase of life when they are growing efficiently on forages, but when they begin to mature and we move them to their feed yard phase, we can better intensely manage them in a way that is best for them and the feed resources that are available.

Cattle are quite miraculous creatures and are very often misunderstood. A world without cattle and other ruminants would be overgrown with weeds and brush and have piles of leftover grains that have little nutritional value to us.

It's Not a Cow. It's a Goat.

All right, I realize that it shouldn't be too hard to tell cattle from goats, but if all you had was a snapshot of their insides (it's what's inside that counts…*ha!*), you'd realize that they are quite similar. That's because cattle and goats are *both* ruminants! But wait, there's more! It's not just that cattle and goats are ruminants but also our longtime human friend, sheep. All of these domesticated animals that "chew their cud" are ruminants.

If you've ever sat glassy-eyed staring at a cow for a long time like I have (that's not weird; *you're* weird!), you'd notice that they seem to be noshing on something at nearly all times, even if they have not recently eaten something. That's because they often are chewing on something called *cud*. Cud is the fibrous feed that they have eaten, which they regurgitate shortly after ingesting it so that they can break it down even more. The grinding action of their molars on these fibrous forages makes the pieces smaller so that more of the bacteria in their gut can attach to it and ferment it.

You'll often see an animal chewing its cud as very relaxed looking, often lying down, but at times standing. This is a bit of an evolutionary response. Cattle and other ruminants are prey animals, as are most herbivores. They seem to have developed this means of additional digestion as a way to better utilize nutrients that otherwise were eaten in haste.

Think of an animal out grazing in the wild in the open. They would be somewhat vulnerable to predators. So cattle and other ruminants are able to eat a lot of feed quickly; store it in their big fermentation vat, the rumen; and then scurry back to a safe place, most likely with their herd mates.

The problem with eating things quickly is that they don't have a chance to break down the feed very well. This is where chewing one's cud comes into place. Cattle and other ruminants, once they feel they are in a safe and calm spot, will often lie down or settle in some way, turn on some Enya (probably not), and calmly begin to regurgitate their feed so that it can be rechewed. Sounds delightful!

Since we're on the topic of prey animals, do you know what other animals would fall under the category of ruminant? Turns out there are a lot of our enteric fermenters that are found in the wild (and semiwild) environments. The close cousin of cattle, the great American bison, is one of the native megafauna of the United States and Canada, and they too are ruminants. Considering they were estimated to have numbered upward of sixty million prior to ethnic Europeans settling North America (with not a feed yard to be had), that's a lot of bison burps that must have been eructated. In comparison, there are around ninety million cattle in the United States. However, those are intensely managed and are a very efficient creature considering the smaller farming and ranching resources in the US each year yet a steady production of meat and milk from those critters.

How about our friends in the Cervidae family? No, I'm not referring to an obscure lineage of Calabrese Italians; I'm talking about deer. It is estimated that there are around thirty million deer (white tail, black tail, and mule deer) in the United States. These critters come in all sizes and shapes and include caribou (reindeer) as well as moose. And by the way, all deer are ruminants.

Other curious ruminants would include mountain goats, bighorn sheep, antelope, water buffalo, and yaks. Cattle, of course, have just held a longer relationship with people than many of the other ruminant creatures. Forage fermenters are all around us; cattle are merely a domesticated descendent of some rather interesting and dynamic animals that we may encounter on our hikes or international travels.

CHAPTER 4

It's Not a Cow—It's... Complicated

In the animal agriculture industry, we realize many people are not involved in agriculture, let alone the animal sector. This is evident by the immense amount of confusion and misinformation being shared about agriculture (faster and faster as communication technologies advance, mind you). As a result, many of us who are committed to telling the story of agriculture have been tasked with developing our "elevator speech."

Now for those who are unfamiliar with elevator speeches, these are not descriptions about how to mechanically relocate a human from one floor to another in a building but rather to be able to explain one's thesis or objective in the time it takes to travel in an elevator, about thirty seconds to possibly a little over a minute (about the attention time of most people, including myself). However, when the disparity in understanding of agriculture is so vast—as what is observed in the modern-day environment of a developed nation such as the United States, where the overwhelming majority of citizens are not at all connected to farming and ranching—you find that thirty to sixty seconds are not at all enough time to explain the cattle production community to them. That's where I finally came to the realization that it's going to take a bit more effort to share the story of animal agriculture, specifically the beef and dairy cattle industries, so let's get to work!

As I've mentioned in earlier chapters, there are a great many definitions of cattle that make up what is found in the bovine community, but that's only the beginning of the complexity of this animal science topic. Cattle specialties can be broken into two main direction: beef (meat) and dairy (milk). Let's focus this chapter on beef.

Beef cattle production in the United States (and most industrialized countries, for that matter) is set up well to optimize resources, efficiency, and efficacy. Okay, let's be real. Most of modern agriculture practices optimize all of those things, but what does that mean? Notice I specifically chose the word *optimize* instead of *maximize*. Think of driving a car. It's been long understood that to optimize speed and fuel economy, driving around fifty-five miles per hour will fulfill that objective. However, one could maximize speed by driving all out, foot to the floor. However, the resources (fuel) would be expended rapidly, and therefore, efficiency would be lost. One could maximize resources (again, fuel). However, that would likely leave you traveling at idle speed, and you wouldn't get very far very fast. What modern agriculture does is optimize the resources while also optimizing the ability to produce safe, reliable, and nutritious food—in this case, milk and meat.

The way that the cattle systems work is that because we're dealing with such a big animal, it makes sense to somewhat specialize as a farmer or rancher. In the beef-production system, that specialization results in four main segments that sometimes have overlaps depending on the farmer or rancher in charge of the herd. Those segments are seed stock, commercial cow-calf, stocker/backgrounder, and feed yard. That's a lot to cover, so let's get started!

Seed stock

When you think of beef cattle production, most probably don't think about the Westminster Kennel Club show. Well, that's because that's a dog show, of course (and dogs and cattle are clearly different; I know that because they are spelled differently). But what if I told you that there are, in fact, shows like that where cattle are the subjects of competition. Not all cattle get to go to fancy shows, but livestock shows are indeed opportunities for cattlemen and women to exhibit their best and compete against others in the cattle world.

In the case of the cattle show, you may be looking at purebred cattle of specific breeds like those talked about earlier. These purebred animals are going to be registered through their respective breed organization (e.g., American Angus Association, American Hereford Association, American Brahman Breeders Association, etc.), where their pedigrees or lineages will be documented.

The documentation of purebred cattle through the breed organizations lend to great opportunities for cattle ranchers in the seed stock sector of the cattle business. These folks look for patterns of certain traits (e.g., muscling, growth potential, mothering characteristics, etc.) for making breeding decisions for the next generation of purebred stock. The breed organizations will compile mountains of data on the calves of those bull and cow/heifer matings to help with the predictability of the next time that those bulls and cows are mated. These data crunchers at the breed organizations have greatly helped to advance the efficiency and efficacy of the cattle herd in the United States as well as other countries where calf data are collected. The massive amounts of data are compiled into more easy-to-understand number indexes called "expected progeny differences" or more commonly referred to as EPDs. Although, as I mentioned, EPDs are somewhat easy to understand. To someone who is less familiar with the idea, it still looks like a bunch of numbers and random abbreviations, but these EPDs are amazing tools that help to improve cattle performance in the next generation.

The old way of selectively breeding cattle involved just looking at the cow and finding a bull that you think might be a good match either appearancewise or by known past performance. Now, because of the advent of EPDs, the decision is much more precise, and the results allow for rapid changes in the cattle herd. This is really important since if a decision to change something in a rancher's herd was made, they have to consider that it takes nine months for the pregnancy of a cow and then about another eighteen months before that calf would be ready to be harvested for meat. A lot can happen in that time frame.

Even more so, the affordability of DNA tests have become so that cattle ranchers can take a DNA sample when a calf is young to look at the potential of its performance, which can also shorten the time it takes to make decisions in one's herd. Customer preferences continue to change, and cattle ranchers are constantly doing their best to provide the best product that they can at a good value. One of the ways to improve product and lower the overall cost of production is to use the technologies at hand that can help make those changes more efficient (and effective).

There's a lot of science being used in the cattle-raising community! As a result, these animals are very valuable and command a price that is according to their potential to raise calves that will be the next great steak. Many of the bulls in the seed stock ranching community will sell from a few thousand dollars to upward of a million dollars for the most elite. Mind you, this is a very select few that sell for the very high amounts, so before you decide to dive into the cattle seed stock business, understand that it's a long way to the top (AC/DC reference!).

These purebred cattle are the foundation of the cattle herd and make the big changes that we may see in what cattle may look like outwardly and how they perform inwardly. The animals in the seed stock sector are primarily used for breeding and are not going to be what is ultimately found as steaks in the local supermarket. Although when the bulls and cows in a seed stock herd eventually become too old or are not what is being considered for what is ideal beef livestock, they will be harvested and most often used for ground beef production. The traditional beef seen in the meat case at your favorite grocery store more likely came from the next step in the chain: the commercial cow-calf ranch.

Commercial cow-calf

The customer of the seed stock rancher is often the commercial cow-calf rancher. These are the majority of cattle operations in the United States and are the heavy lifters of the ranching community in that nearly all of the beef found in the supermarket and on a plate in a restaurant will begin at one of these ranches. Commercial cow-calf establishments definitely focus on high-quality genetics that can be obtained from the seed stock ranchers.

However, they are also very much at the mercy of the environment in which the ranch is located. I recall visiting a ranch in Northern Utah one time where the cattle folks were talking about how they considered buying high-quality bull from out of the area who had a lot of potential for growth, but because he wasn't raised for "walking over sagebrush," as they say, he was not ideal for the environment of the area.

Contrary to that, I spent a lot of time in Ohio, which has abundant feed and resources but can get a little soggy during certain times of the year. A tall and big-framed creature would just sink out of sight in that soft ground. Thankfully, the seed stock ranching families are all over the country, producing cows and bulls that can help fill the need of the herds in the commercial cow-calf sector.

The commercial cow-calf ranches most certainly raise a lot of their own heifers and cows and will rely on seed stock cows to help bolster the herd while using the superior genetics of seed stock bulls to help improve their herd. However, the main product out of commercial cow-calf ranches is the steer calf. Of course, they aren't born steers. That usually happens around month two or three of life when the calf is still very young. These calves will be raised with their mothers for somewhere between five to six months, when they will first nurse but then learn from their mothers to eat grass and other forages.

Commercial cow-calf ranches rely greatly on the seasons. It is important for a cow, when she has a calf, to have plenty of feed resources to be able to maintain and grow that calf. Most beef calves will be between eighty and one hundred pounds when they are born. That means that the mamma cow (yes, we do call them mamma cows) needs to make enough milk to keep that baby calf full and growing. Beef cows don't make nearly as much milk as dairy cows, but that's to come. Cows on a *commercial* farm or ranch are usually considered important employees to the family business. As such, they need to be able to have the resources needed to produce (i.e., raise a calf).

The majority of beef cows in North America calve, or give birth, in the late winter and early spring. This allows for the cow to have the highly nutritious and abundant grass that grow well during that time of the year in northern latitudes, such as a lot of the United States. Cattle ranchers still work very closely with Mother Nature to do what is best for the animals and to optimize (there's that word again) resources in a way that is good for the cow and good for the land. This is not a new concept. Quite the contrary. Cattle farmers and ranchers have been in tuned with the seasons for many, many years. It works. If it ain't broke, don't fix it.

When the grass start to fade is usually around the time that the calves are weaned from their mammas. Anyone who has weaned a child from the bottle knows this can be a slightly traumatic experience. That's why a lot of cattle ranchers have looked into ways of minimizing this stress on the calves (and the cows). One way of doing this is called fence-line weaning. This is where the cows are separated from the calves by a fence, usually wire of some sort, so that they can see each other and still touch noses and hang out. However, what we find is that the mamma cows are often the first ones to quickly lose interest, and they will gently walk away after a day or so and get on with their lives. The weaned calves will soon do the same.

We must realize that this is a natural thing that will happen whether we farmers and ranchers intervene or not. The cow's natural instinct is to eventually allow the calf to go off on its own. It's just important that in order to have a sustainable cattle business model, we need to realize that timing is still important. We need to allow for that cow to have a little downtime before she is ready to raise her next calf, and the weaning process is part of that progression of things.

The weaned calves may remain on the ranch in which they were born for a period of time, or they will move on to the next group of ranchers called stockers and backgrounders.

Stockers and backgrounders

When calves are weaned from their mammas, it's because they are physically ready to go off and eat on their own without the need for milk from the cow, and what a big step this can be. These calves at this phase in their life—although they are really only around six months old, chronologically speaking—are more like teenagers, physiologically speaking. They will most likely travel with their herd mates that they grew up with and be allowed to continue what they were already taught to do alongside their mammas: graze. The stocker and backgrounder cattle rancher is one who is also very in tune with the land and forages that are grown on it. That's because what the cattle ranchers are doing in this part of the cattle production cycle is using the *teenageness* of the weaned calves to grow on relatively inexpensive feed: grass!

Being a cattle stocker rancher, the idea is mostly being a pasture manager and harvester of sunlight. A semiadolescent/semiadult steer is going to grow similar to our early teenage humans. You could feed them just about anything, and they'll grow. I joke that as a teenager, my mother could have fed me nothing but lettuce and ice cubes, and I'd still grow. Of course, she didn't feed me lettuce and ice cubes, but you get the picture.

Mammalian animals, including cattle, during the adolescent phase of life are amazing growing machines. The cattle ranching community knows this well and use it to their advantage since, again, cattle are ruminants and can turn grass that have no nutritional value to us into muscle that we can then harvest as meat. Oftentimes, these stocker ranches are going to be found in similar areas that the cow-calf ranches are also found since forage is still the main feed that these animals are going to be eating. There's a chance that the calves will also receive a little bit of supplemental protein and minerals in the form of a grain mixture, but most of the time, cattle in a stocker situation are out doing what they do very well, and that's grazing.

Grazing land can be the pastures that are unsuitable for growing crops but can also be what's left over after a crop is removed. Stubble and crop residue from grain production can be used as a feed source, and the cattle can also help the farmer by cleaning up more of the organic matter left behind after a grain crop is harvested.

Being a cattle stocking rancher, one has to, of course, be good at managing the pasture and grazing resources but also have to be good at building and maintaining fences. In some cases, it's miles upon miles of fencing. This is important as cattle are great at being turned out into vast and wide-open spaces and will find the grass and forages they need to eat and grow, but it's also important to be able to collect those cattle at the end of the growing season or if there's an issue and a rancher needs to help the animals in some way or another. Fencing also protects the animals from wandering into areas that otherwise would put them and people into potential harm, such as roadways or residential areas. But really, cattle could be working hard right where you drive every day, and because they are behind the trees or a hill, you may not know they are there.

Now I've mentioned stocking and backgrounding, and although they are very similar, they are still a little different. Backgrounding usually involves the feed and forages being brought to the cattle and not the cattle having to go find the feed and forages. This idea is for either areas of the country that do not produce enough grass to sustain a herd of cattle, so the feed is brought in from other areas that grow it better, or it's for times of the year when grass just aren't growing.

Backgrounding calves may happen with animals that have been born at a time of year that by the time they are old enough to be weaned and go out on their own, the grass in pasture and rangeland are no longer available. This is where the calves can be fed hay and other relatively inexpensive feed and still grow in a way that would be similar to how their counterparts would have grown on pasture. The calves in a backgrounding scenario would likely be introduced to some grain or starch in their diet to help them grow that much more, and so they get used to the starches, which will become much more important in the feed yard phase.

Stocking and backgrounding farms and ranches are important parts of the cattle industry as they also can act as a shock absorber to the amount of cattle that are being raised in North America. The majority of beef calves born in the United States every year are born between the months of January and April. These are called "spring calves." However, because there is a big supply of calves all at one time yet we need to have beef in restaurants and grocery stores year-round, it is important to meter out the amount of cattle being *finished* prior to being harvested. I'll mention finishing here in a little bit, but the point being that by using nature's cycle of good grass-growing conditions during the spring and summer allows for this *glut* of calves to evenly make their way to the final phase of beef production the feeding phase.

Finishing

As the name implies, finishing is the last step prior to steers being harvested for meat, but it's far from what many would consider the end-of-days scenario for cattle—quite the contrary. An unfortunate thing about the overwhelming majority of people in developed countries, like the United States, from being several generations separated from agriculture is that it allows for imaginations to run wild about things that are less understood. Those who are opposed to modern agricultural practices, or simply who do not know the how and why we do things in agriculture, have come to some conclusions that are very unproductive and, in many cases, outright incorrect. These folks have painted agriculture, especially animal agriculture, in a very dire scene. Cattle farming and ranching, I believe, has become one of the biggest targets to the anti-ag crowd, and at the bull's-eye are the feed yards used in the finishing part of the beef cattle lifecycle. So let's address some of the concerns and shine light on the subject that has been given such a black eye.

Yes, it is true that cattle at a finishing farm or ranch are destined for harvest. Their days at the feed yard are maintained as best as we humans can provide while also optimizing resources. Feed yards, as the name implies, are farms or ranches where we bring groups of cattle that are beginning to reach physical maturity, and we feed them in an intensively managed way.

In order to optimize the feed resources, feed yards will have nutritionists who formulate very well-balanced diets that are made so that the cattle can grow efficiently and effectively while being financially sustainable. Oftentimes, ruminant nutritionists are well-educated animal scientists who have either a master's degree or PhD in the subject of animal digestion and nutrition. This means that they are meticulously precise in what the diets of the cattle are composed of and how they are made.

Although the ruminant nutritionist is more than likely not the person actually mixing the feed and giving it to the cattle, they are the ones making the big decisions on what will actually be fed. Think of them as the executive chef making the recipes for a big hotel or banqueting center. The executive chef may indeed do a bit of cooking, but it's the sous-chefs and line cooks who really make the meals. However, one needs to have the top lead making the big decisions, and that's what the ruminant nutritionist does.

So what exactly is it that the cattle eat? Feed yards make up a recipe called a "total mixed ration." Sounds fancy and scientific. Well, it is quite scientific, but if you take a close look at what is in a total mixed ration, or TMR for short, you can actually pick out the specific ingredients that make up the meal. Total mixed rations look a bit like trail mix where you take a bunch of whole tasty ingredients, each with their own unique nutritional properties, and mix them up so that each handful (or mouthful, if you're cattle) has everything in it. Although TMRs don't contain raisins or chocolate chips (except for when they do), they most often are made up of some chopped hay, grain (corn, wheat, barley, etc.), a vegetable source of protein (soybeans or distiller's grains), and likely some supplemental vitamins and minerals.

Sometimes, instead of hay or in combination with it, the cattle are fed silage. Silage is a chopped feed that is made from the whole stalk of a grass or plant that is then packed into enormous bags, bunkers, or silos and is allowed to ferment. Silage is similar to sauerkraut where it is high moisture, slightly acidic, and delicious (at least to cattle)! Silage is cattle kimchi. The cool thing about silage is that not only do cattle love it, but it is also very nutritious and a great component to a TMR.

Rations are often mixed in either big stationary mixers or mixer trucks. These mixers are like giant versions of what you may see in a commercial bakery. Big trucks can mix and chop the ingredients of the TMR and then are able to deliver the meal to the hungry diners (i.e., cattle).

It is very true that cattle in feed yards are in pens, but let's put some context to that. The pens are enormous, usually have a big mound of dirt for cattle to climb and hang out on, and still certainly allow for cattle to exhibit natural behavior. Anyone who says otherwise has either clearly not been to a feed yard or only has ever seen pictures or videos of feed yards severely edited and taken out of context. Feed yards work with cattle's natural behavior of being herd animals. They are also places where incredible care is taken with regard to health and well-being. I know this may sound a bit wild, but I often equate them to all-inclusive resorts. Just bear with me as I explain.

If you've ever been to an all-inclusive resort or on a cruise, what is it that you do? You eat, you sleep, you hang out with your friends. Well, let's look at the feed yard situation. The meals are prepared by people who have been advised by nutritionists with doctorates in the field of animal digestion. The meals are also highly palatable, as in the cattle really like how the feed tastes. The cattle can eat all that they want. However, when they are full, they can go take a nap or ruminate or both as they see fit. The cattle hang out with their friends. Cattle are herd animals.

They are also prey animals. They have no interest in being out in wide-open spaces alone. In fact, if you put a large group of cattle out in a thousand-acre pasture, they still bunch up. Feed yards give cattle plenty of room in the pens to move around, play, and socialize. Many people who are unfamiliar with feed yards think that the cattle have no room to move and are chained in place where they are force fed. *Way off!* If you are a person who has been fortunate enough to go to a resort or on a cruise, even though the resorts have gyms, plenty of physical activities to engage in, and you have the option of eating salad and cucumbers, what is it that you do? You eat the tasty food, you hang out with friends, and you take naps—*and* you paid to do it! So far so good?

Another thing about feed yards that is misunderstood is just how content the cattle are. Animal behavioralists, especially those familiar with livestock, will tell you that if cattle are content, they rarely vocalize and will be rather quiet. I've been in the middle of feed yards where there are many pens of cattle, totaling upward of fifty thousand animals, and the yard is nearly silent. The only sound you hear is maybe a truck off in the distance or the clinking of a chain on fence that a curious steer is investigating—but no mooing, a sign of good animal welfare and content critters, not at all unusual but rather the norm.

What about the poop? Uh-oh, somebody's about to talk s———. It shouldn't come as a surprise that cattle in feed yards do sometimes sit down in their own poop. That's because—wait for it—they're animals! Cattle especially are rather unconcerned with this. Again, something they would probably do in an open field. A perfect example was just the other day. I was watching my own steers, which have a big green pasture to frolic about in to their hearts content. They were, however, hanging out under a small shelter that we provide for them. They were in the shelter ruminating, and one was casually defecating right where it would probably sleep that evening. It's not that they didn't have a whole field to go out in. It's that they really couldn't care less.

But back to the feed yards, the pens are monitored for the accumulation of manure and are regularly cleaned out before new cattle are brought in. Manure generated in feed yards has actually become a sought-after commodity. The manure is composted and has great value as such, which can be sold outright or used on neighboring fields of crops to add nutrients into the soils and help to grow the next batch of feed. It's a brilliant, beefy cycle!

A really neat observation I have had the opportunity of experiencing is on some of the feed yards that are catering to the customer who is adamant about cattle needing to have pasture to graze at all times. These feed yards still mix rations similar to the rest of the cattle in traditional pen settings. However, the cattle have the option of grazing if they choose to do so. It's always interesting to bring folks to those yards who have not worked with cattle much. What they see generally is that the cattle hang out in the areas where the feed bunks (big troughs) are waiting for the next installment of TMR. The cattle prefer the TMR to grazing the grass. The mixed feed is tasty to them, more so than the grass in the field. Again, back to the resort example, you have the option of the appetizing high-calorie deserts and decadent food, or you can graze at the salad bar on your vacation. Which would you prefer?

Feed yards also often have either a consulting veterinarian who works very closely with the operation, or they have one actually on staff if the feed yard is big enough to warrant one. Not much different than a resort or cruise that almost always have medical professionals on-site to help out in case there are illnesses.

Of course, the end goal is to grow the cattle to a sizable weight (around 1,400 pounds) so that they can be harvested for meat. That's definitely where the resort similarities end, but let's talk about that last step to get the steak on the plate.

CHAPTER 5

It's Not a Cow—It's Delicious!

Beef! It's what's for dinner! However, a wise man once told me that there are at least twenty-one opportunities a week to eat beef (thanks, Dr. Scanga!). Beef satisfies like no other protein. It's not only a wholesome and humble treat in ground or country-fried form, but it's also decadent and luxurious when described with a French flair like *filet* or *chateau*. Beef has long been considered a very tasty delicacy, and it does, in fact, satisfy.

After the journey of growing a beef steer from a small calf on a ranch, through the stocking phase, and finishing at around 1,400 pounds, you're looking at nearly two years of effort. Yet because of the amazing job that the farming and ranching community has done, beef is both affordable and available. However, it's rarely the cheaper buy. Most often, pork and poultry can satisfy the meat tooth's cravings, but beef brings a dimension and depth of flavor to which the other domesticated denizens of the barnyard can't compare.

Unlike pork and poultry, however, beef does come with a bit of variability and is a much larger animal, which brings about other challenges when it comes to ultimately getting that big beast into steaks and burgers. That's where the noble craft of the butcher becomes an essential task to transition the large ruminant into roastable form.

The harvesting process

There's much debate in the meat animal community as to what we should call this next step. I will forewarn that those who choose to not read this section of how we turn a live animal into a beef carcass should probably skip to the next section in this chapter. For those with interest, however, we should first consider the terminology. For many years, folks in the meat processing community call the slaughtering of animals the "harvesting process." It's a great term and truly describes what is being done: we're harvesting a crop that we've grown.

However, there are certainly some who say that we've sanitized the step in the meat-production system to the point that we've lost the meaning and are not acknowledging the fact that we are indeed taking an animal's life in the pursuit of food. We have been doing this for quite some time as humans, albeit I think we've come a long way from running bison over a cliff and have greatly improved the process for the animal's sake as well as for ours.

For the longest time, killing animals for food in society was simply referred to as *slaughter*, and I will use that and *harvest* interchangeably going forward. I can see the argument of toning down the descriptor and saying harvest for those who like to enjoy meat but don't need to hear the details. I can also understand why some say that it's important to remind us that we are indeed taking an animal's life so that we can survive and that using the term *slaughter* is acknowledging that life itself is messy at times. Either way, as I once heard someone say, "You have to kill the chicken to get the chicken out of the chicken." Well, same with beef.

Most folks who are not familiar with the process of slaughtering an animal are often very intrigued with it and may have preconceived notions. A lot think of the act of slaughtering an animal will be similar to a horror movie resulting in a violent and explosive death. However, when done correctly, it is a rather uneventful and systematic process. It is important that the animal does not suffer—for the animal's sake first, for the safety of the people doing the actual job of harvesting the animal second, and ultimately for the quality of the meat.

In order for meat to be salable, the process of harvesting the animal and the subsequent cutting of the meat must be done under inspection, either state or federal. This means that the meat is deemed wholesome and safe for consumption.

The first step in the commercial harvesting process actually begins with what is called *antemortem* inspection. A food safety official, often a veterinarian but could also be a USDA meat inspector, will evaluate the live animal for any signs of disease or illness. Once the animal is deemed fit for harvest, the animal is walked calmly from the holding pen into the harvesting facility. Holding pens at a harvesting facility are designed where the animal cannot hurt itself and has access to water at all times. Not only is this the right thing to do for the animal, it's also the law. Animals that are held overnight must be given feed. However, this is a rare occurrence. Cattle normally are at a packing plant for about two hours, which allows for them to relax after the trip (usually a couple of hours or less in a livestock trailer) before being led into the harvesting facility.

Animal handling and movement is done in a very calm and quiet manner. Gone are the days of whooping and hollering to move animals. And most packing houses have completely eliminated the use of electric prods to the extent that many commercial facilities do not even have one on premises. We just keep getting better and better at understanding how cattle behave, and over the past several decades, dramatic improvements have been made in facility design and employee management. Dr. Temple Grandin and Dr. Lily Edwards-Callaway in the Department of Animal Sciences at Colorado State University are some of the world's leading experts in packing plant design to minimize stress and optimize animal well-being. The majority of large-scale commercial packing houses in the world have been influenced by Dr. Grandin's designs, and Dr. Edwards-Callaway continues the mission of improved animal handling with her experience in both academia but also industry. The influence of these amazing ladies and others like them in the field of animal behavioral studies continue to improve the welfare of meat animals while also improving the safety of the people who work with the livestock.

From the pens, cattle are walked into a single-file chute where they are eventually led to what is called the "knock box." In large-scale harvesting facilities, the infrastructure allows for something called a "center-track restrainer" chute that actually gently lifts the animal off of the ground by using a metal conveyor belt of sorts, which allows the steer to rest its breast bone on the belt. The cattle essentially feel a little weightless as the belt moves them along in a very gentle and slow manner. The sides of the chute are solid so they are not distracted by anything or anyone on the other side of the chute. At the end of the chute will be the individual who has the task of rendering the animal unconscious prior to it being bled out. Again, it's the right thing to do, and it's the law![3]

Knocking a beef animal in a commercial meat-packing facility is almost entirely done in using what is called a captive bolt gun. This means that a bolt or smooth metal rod is fired into the brain of the animal using either a gunpowder cartridge (like a.22 blank) or is operated pneumati-

---

[3] An exception to the rule of rendering cattle unconscious is what's called "religious exemption." Religious exemption means that if there are reasons why a certain religious practice prevents the animal from being rendered unconscious prior to bleeding, then this can be the done as an alternative to the normal traditional practice. A specific example is the traditional kosher slaughter. Slaughter done under kosher exemption requires the animal to be conscious when the fatal wound is inflicted. This is done under extremely controlled circumstances and by very skilled practitioners of the Jewish faith known as shochets. The understanding is that because of the immense loss of blood at bleeding, the animal goes into shock very quickly and is therefore unconscious as the bleed-out occurs. Some halal (*lawful* under the Islamic tradition) product is from animals harvested in a similar manner.

cally (high-pressure air). As opposed to a firearm, like a rifle or pistol, a captive bolt gun controls the bolt that is fired, and it never fully leaves the gun as a projectile. The bolt is retracted after it is fired by the use of springs or rubber O-rings. This makes the use of the device very safe for the person using it.

When used properly, the captive bolt gun renders the animal unconscious instantly. The unconscious cattle are then hoisted up by the hind leg using a chain on a winch or continuous-moving rail system, where the animal can then be safely bled. Hoisting cattle that have been rendered unconscious will allow for gravity to help with the proper bleeding of the carcass. Although the animal is brain-dead, the heart will still beat for a few minutes, which will help with the bleeding out as well.

After the animal is rendered unconscious and hoisted up by the hind leg, there may be some uncoordinated kicking of the free hind leg. This is very normal. What is happening is that the nerves that control the legs are in the spine, and when the brain is no longer functioning, it is not uncommon to have some short-circuiting of the nerves, which causes some movement in a free hind leg. The animal is not conscious and is definitely not coming back to life. It's merely a physiological response to the lack of control from the brain any longer.

I must mention that there are videos out there that are shown by people who do not like that we harvest cattle (or any animal for that matter) for meat. They show these otherwise benign videos of packing houses out of context and say that cattle are hoisted up by their hind leg while they are still alive. They are not alive, but to the unknowing viewer, it may look unnatural. Although, from an academic sense, the stunned cattle may have some circulation still going on in the body due to the heart still beating for that short time after the stun, the animal does not feel a thing and is technically brain-dead.

There are ways that animal behavior and animal welfare specialists have identified to help slaughterhouses know that they are stunning cattle correctly. They must look for signs of a floppy head, often with the tongue sticking out and flaccid; no rhythmic eye movement; no coordinated breathing; and most importantly, no righting reflex. The righting reflex is if the animal is trying to lift its head upward toward its back and arching its back in an effort to stand. United States Department of Agriculture (USDA) inspectors monitor the stunning process in a meat animal harvesting facility to be sure that this process is being done correctly every time at all times. One more time, it's the right thing to do, and it's the law!

After the cattle are rendered unconscious, it is important to bleed it quickly. Bleeding, also known as *exsanguination*, is done shortly after the cattle are lifted up by their hind leg. A sharp knife is inserted into the hide of the neck between the animal's lower jaw and its breastbone. This knife is then either exchanged for a clean knife, or the same knife is sanitized quickly with extremely hot water, and then the person doing the exsanguination will reach in through the incision and cut into the lower part of the neck to sever the carotid artery and jugular vein. This allows for an efficient and effective release of blood from the body of the cattle. Full-grown cattle will release over five gallons of blood during the bleeding process in a slaughterhouse. That's a lot! The amount of blood produced during the bleeding process is about three percent of the live weight of the animal. Amazingly, this will remove over ninety percent of the blood from the body of the cattle, which is important as blood left in the meat will lead to rapid spoilage and quality issues.

Blood is captured in large-scale facilities and often dried and sold as fertilizer and feed sources for other animals. Beef blood is not generally used for human food, but it is still used, nonetheless. In fact, pretty much every part of cattle carcasses finds a use. It is important that we honor the life of the animals we harvest by fully utilizing its pieces and parts. The hide is of course sent for leather processing. It's really unfortunate that we don't use and wear more leather items as it is a naturally produced material that is flexible and extremely durable.

The bones of the carcass will be ground and also used as an amazing animal mineral supplement for pet food and other livestock feed such as chickens and hogs. The organs are primarily sold as offal meats. Most organ meats are going to be sold in ethnic markets in the United States or exported to countries that have a demand for those cuts. The palate of most United States citizens is just not one that craves the intense flavors and textures of tripe (rumen and stomach), liver, heart, and kidney, but thankfully, there are many that do, and US cattle are able to fill that desire.

I would say, however, that there is a bit of a resurgence in the interest of what are called "variety meats" (organ meats), and hopefully, we do continue to see demand increase domestically. The intestines of the animals, however, do certainly have a demand as the interest in old-world salamis continue to increase worldwide. When made traditionally, the intestines are what the salamis are encased in.

One thing that is generated in large amounts during the harvesting and subsequent cutting, also known as *fabrication*, of the carcass is fat. Beef fat has a unique property compared to pork and chicken fat in that it is more solid in texture and makeup. That has to do with how ruminants digest food and deposit fats as a result. Sheep, goats, etc. also have fats that are more solid at room temperatures.

These fats are used for a variety of things. First, it's used as an ingredient in ground beef production. Ground beef receives a lot of its flavor from the fat that is included in it. A higher fat percentage in ground beef will generally result in a more flavorful and juicier burger. Of course, the higher fat content in ground beef needs to be balanced, depending on the ultimate application. If one is making a pasta sauce and prefers to have the meat a bit leaner, then we need to look at a bit of a different use for the fat generated from the beef carcass.

Beef fat has been used in the past for deep-fat frying and baking, but these uses have fallen out of fashion in lieu of vegetable oils. The excess beef fat that cannot be merchandised as food will go through a rendering process and will be used for the creation of industrial lubricants, soaps, candles, cosmetic bases, and more and more are finding their way to biodiesel production. Again, one way or another, nearly every part of the harvested animal is used, and that's a good thing.

Beef grades

The primary objective of harvesting a beef animal is, of course, the red meat. The special taste of beef meat has long been sought after by humanity and still is today, but it has become a complicated subject in its own right. Most beef in the United States (and similarly in Canada), once the carcass is chilled down over a twenty-four-hour period, will be assessed a grade to identify its potential eating quality and value.

For most folks reading this, the quality grade of beef is going to be the primary deciding factor for the cost-value relationship that they will consider when purchasing a piece of beef. In the United States there are officially eight quality grades of beef that can be assessed by USDA personnel. However, the overwhelming majority of beef that is assessed a grade will be within one of three categories: USDA Select, USDA Choice, and USDA Prime.[4]

---

[4] The eight official USDA grades of beef from order of highest value and eating quality to lowest are Prime, Choice, Select, Standard, Commercial, Utility, Cutter, and Canner. The first four grades (Prime, Choice, Select, Standard) can be assigned to carcasses that are from younger cattle—generally speaking, less than thirty months of age. The remaining four USDA grades can be assigned to older cattle (greater than thirty months of age). Age is generally determined by dentition in the packing house on the harvesting floor after the animal has been bled. In the past, age of beef was determined by an estimation based on the skeletal structure of the vertebrae on the carcass. Bone maturity estimation has not been used in large quantity ever since 2017 when USDA approved the use of

One could think of this as a "good, better, best" scenario. These different grades of beef are influenced greatly by the amount of marbling that they contain. What is marbling you ask? Well, I'm excited to tell you!

Marbling, in supersimple terms, are little flecks of fat (what I often call little flecks of flavor) that are interspersed in the muscle of the meat found on a beef carcass. Actually, marbling is in other species as well. It just receives a lot of focus when it comes to beef. Marbling fat is a little different from other fats found in the beef carcass such as back fat (subcutaneous) or visceral (abdominal) fat.

Marbling has been observed to contain a bit more monounsaturated fats than the other fat depots in the carcass. Monounsaturated fats are not only really tasty, but they are also good for you—*yay beef!* One monounsaturated fat in particular, oleic acid, is found in high quantities in olive oil, sunflower seeds, avocados, and—wait for it— beef marbling! Interesting how nature designed it so that a nutrient that is good for you is also often really tasty. But beyond the oleic acid, marbling contains a number of other flavor compounds that give beef it's unique taste. Science has shown that as marbling increases, so does the overall eating experience of beef.

The USDA beef quality grades focus on marbling, and as marbling amount increases, so does the beef grade.

---

dentition for age determination. The reality is that mostly USDA Prime, Choice, and Select are assigned to beef carcasses even though there are five other grades. The overwhelming majority (over ninety percent) of all beef carcasses harvested in the US will fall within the first three grades, and therefore, it really doesn't pay to even bother using a USDA grader for assigning a grade other than those three.

Marbling is assessed on the beef carcass by USDA graders. These impartial meat quality experts allow for a third-party investigation of the meat quality and value. The USDA grader makes their determination of marbling in the beef carcass at the same location on each carcass. That's done at a cut between the twelfth and thirteenth rib bones on the carcass back, which exposes a big muscle of great value: the rib eye! The rib eye muscle is evaluated for marbling content, and the approximate fat percentage of USDA Select, Choice, and Prime are around 3.5 percent, 5.0 percent, and 8.5 percent, respectively. These incremental increases in flecks of fat allow for different eating experiences and, therefore, different value propositions.

Not long ago, there was a lot of USDA Select beef available. A lot has happened in the cattle raising community, however, and between serendipitous natural events and intentional breeding decisions on the part of cattle ranchers, the amount of beef carcasses receiving the higher grades of beef (Choice and Prime) have increase greatly, and the amount of Select has decreased as a percentage. This is not by accident. Nobody makes higher quality anything unless there's a greater value assigned to it. It turns out that cattle ranchers have realized that the consuming public is okay with the higher marbling in the meat, and they enjoy it. In fact, they enjoy it to the point that they are willing to pay more for it. But before the skeptics say, "Well, that's just the American palate," let's consider other countries that are assigning premiums to the higher marbled cattle carcasses.

First, let's look at a system that is very similar to that of the United States when it comes to assigning value to marbling fat: oh, Canada! The Canadian Beef Grading Agency does the job that is similar to that of our USDA in the United States. So similar that they indeed use the same marbling standards as the US. In general, Canada Prime is nearly identical to USDA Prime. Then things get a little different in name, but in name alone. In Canada, a grade nearly the same as USDA Choice is Canada AAA (pronounced "triple A"). Yes, there's a bad Canadian joke in there somewhere (A, eh?). The equivalent of USDA Select is Canada AA and so on. Canada certainly brings in some very fine nuances to their grading system as well, like fat color standards, etc., but you get the point. Canada's value for beef marbling is very similar to that of the US.

Many have come to realize that the Japanese have created some magnificent cattle for beef purposes. The terms *Kobe* and *Wagyu*, to those in the know, have come to mean decadent and rich beef-eating experiences. Kobe, Japan, is an area in that country that is known for its super-high-quality beef, beef specifically from Wagyu cattle. Wagyu cattle, as mentioned earlier in the cattle breeds section, are specifically bred to have high-marbling potential.

However, just like all biological creatures, not all are created exactly the same. Variation does exist in the Wagyu cattle breed, and as such, for those to be considered special, they must go through the Japanese grading system evaluation. This is a similar assessment to the US system. However, the evaluation is done at a cross section between the sixth and seventh ribs of the carcass to expose the rib eye steak muscle. This is where marbling goes into orbit, and the potential for Wagyu cattle to marble is out of this world! These cattle have been bred over many generations to focus on marbling, which is why the Japanese grading system looks at marbling standards that reach well into the double digits of fat percentages in the rib eye muscle.

A top-level marbling assessment of the Japanese grading system, *A5*, would mean that the carcass is trim and well-muscled ("A") and has a very high degree of marbling ("5"). What I often find a little funny is how much people value the term A5 and fail to realize that the letter in A5 really has nothing to do with eating quality; it only tells you how much meat a butcher should expect to get off of the carcass as opposed to fat and bone. I've never had the chance to purchase a Wagyu carcass in Japan, but if I could, I would probably put a lot less value on the letter (A, highest amount of meat as a percentage of the carcass; C, lowest amount of meat as a percentage of the carcass) and really focus on the number. In this case, the higher the number, the higher the amount of magical marbling!

The final major grading system we'll discuss when it comes to marbling value is that of Australia. In fact, from a meat science perspective, Australia's grading system is probably one of the most precise and scientific (of course, that can lead to complications in educating consumers). But yet again, the Australians put value on the incremental increases in marbling as it relates to potential eating quality. Australians also consider breed type, finishing feed regime, muscle pH (really big deal in meat science), and whether or not the animal received growth-promoting technologies.

All really important for estimating eating quality potential, but the big contributing factor that I would say influences the eating quality the most on the carcass will be the marbling yet again.

I would be remiss to leave out the grading system used by countries of the European Union. This system, however, from a meat science perspective, misses the mark when it comes to providing value to marbling fat. The SEUROP (I pronounce it *S-EUROP*, but I've also heard it pronounced like the word *syrup*) standards used in the European Union for beef grading and value assessment really look at muscling of the beef carcass and possibly the outer fat layers; marbling just doesn't receive much attention. However, I would say, based on personal experience working with meat experts in Europe, that there definitely is interest in focusing on more marbling potential in cattle raised on that continent. Time will tell if those standards are modified to fit the palate of beef connoisseurs.

Beef cuts

This can be a massive topic. I've often been asked, "How many steaks can you get out of a beef carcass?"

And of course, being the smart aleck that I am, I always answer, "Well, it depends on how thin you cut them." *Ha!*

Honestly, the real answer will always depend on how you go about fabricating the carcass. Fabricating, although it sounds counterintuitive, is the term used in the meat cutting world for actually cutting up the carcass into smaller, more user-friendly pieces. Let's start with the primals.

Primals are the major cuts, or *breaks*, on a carcass. In the case of the beef carcass, there are eight classical primals: chuck, rib, loin, round, brisket, shank, plate, and flank. More contemporarily, there are only seven beef primals as the shank is now considered an extension of the chuck. But in all, this is the beginning of the fabrication of the smaller cuts.

The chuck is the big shoulder area that is separated from the rib between the fifth and sixth ribs of the carcass. Ribs are numbered one through thirteen on a side of beef (half of a carcass) and number one is the rib closest to the head of the animal. The chuck is also separated from the brisket primal near the point of the sternum or breastbone. The rib is separated from the loin section at the twelfth and thirteenth rib interface, which also happens to be the location where marbling is assessed on a beef carcass for grading purposes. The plate is a big section of rib bones and cartilage near where the navel of the animal would have been and is separated from the rib at a point depending on how big the short ribs are to be cut (to be discussed). The loin is cut near where the hip bone and the large long bone in the round, the femur, are attached. The flank is separated from the base of the loin.

Chuck. The chuck is what I consider the most succulent of the beef primals. The upper shoulder region of the beef carcass will harbor great amounts of fat that is rich in flavor and works very well with the slow roasting items that come from it. The chuck is cut into two main pieces what are considered *subprimals* or smaller primal cuts. The two major subprimals of the chuck are the chuck roll and the shoulder clod.

The chuck roll is the inner portion of the shoulder, whereas the chuck clod is the outer *arm* portion of the shoulder. The chuck roll is where we can then cut our very traditional chuck pot roasts, but we can also gain amazing cuts like chuck short ribs. The chuck roll also has some newer cuts that are able to be prepared as steaks and include things like chuck eye steaks and, one of my favorites, the Denver steak. Cuts from the chuck roll will often have a bunch of delicious marbling and will also lend themselves well to the slow cooker. Folks need to be a little careful trying to grill all items from the chuck as it is an area of the animal where a lot of movement and strength comes from, but there are also some really tender bites in there as well.

The chuck clod on the outer shoulder has some pretty special cuts in it. The classic chuck clod has three major muscles that are also considered subprimals: the clod heart (not really a heart but is mostly made up of the triceps muscle, the top blade, and the chuck shoulder tender). Interestingly, all three of the muscles were traditionally part of chuck roasts that were stewed or slow cooked, but in more recent years, we have found that they can be quite tender pieces of meat. The clod heart is a nice roast or can be cut into steaks, called ranch steaks, that eat similarly to a top sirloin steak.

The chuck shoulder tender—which is more often known in the meat cutting world by its scientific muscle name, which is the teres major—is so tender that it is often used as an alternative to tenderloin in some cases. However, the biggest success out of the shoulder clod in recent years is the top blade. When cut in a particular manner, it can become what is known as the flat iron steak, and *voilà*, it becomes one of the most tender steaks in the whole carcass, second only to the tenderloin! With a little extra knife work, the chuck has become an awesome source of great steaks and flavorful and affordable roasts.

Brisket. What can I say about the brisket? Well, turns out, I can say a lot, considering it's a pretty small beef primal, relatively speaking. The brisket is one of the "thin meats," which also include the classical shank primal, the plate, and the flank. However, contemporarily speaking, the brisket is not all that thin. This primal really has one major subprimal that comes from it: the boneless brisket.

The boneless brisket is made up of two muscles, the deep pectoral called the "brisket flat" and the superficial pectoral, which is called the "brisket point." The brisket muscles do a lot of work moving the front legs of cattle, and as a result, they aren't necessarily very tender as meat cuts. However, if prepared in a slow-cooked method such as traditional barbecue or as corned beef, the brisket can become quite tender.

The tenderness challenges that the brisket has inherently are due to the collagen (chewy stuff) that is throughout those hardworking pectoral muscles. Historically, the brisket would have become fodder for those less fiscally endowed. However, more recently, quality brisket barbecue has become almost a gourmet delight. The brisket flat is often sold as the *lean* cut, while the point (my favorite) is found as the *fat* or *moist* cut. Moreover, smoked brisket has come to be synonymous with Texas cuisine, although there are certainly other regions that lay claim to the cut as well.

Regardless of where or how one enjoys brisket, it is almost always a treat that can be shared with good friends and a good beer (or even a marginal beer for that matter… mmm, beer).

Rib. The rib primal has probably one of the most popular cuts of beef that is both prepared as a steak or a roast: the rib eye. As a steak, the rib eye lends itself to a rich and succulent robust eating experience. It is often found in a boneless form. However, when a bone is left on the cut, it regularly pleases with its curvilinear eye appeal. What's the difference between a bone-in and a boneless rib eye steak, you may ask? Well, the bone, of course.

As far as eating experience there's really not much of a difference. Blasphemous talk, you say! Well, sorry, but this has been demonstrated scientifically that in a blind tasting, people cannot tell any flavor differences between a bone-in and a boneless steak, holding all other parameters constant, of course. A bone, however, is a good insulator, and as a result, the meat right next to the bone of a bone-in steak will likely be a lower degree of doneness than the rest of the steak.

Different degrees of doneness have been observed to produce a different tenderness and flavor, so maybe the sliver of meat near the bone will indeed taste different than the remainder of the steak, however, likely rather inconsequential. It has long been thought that it's the marrow in the bone that gives the bone-in steak more flavor. However, marrow does not leach through the hard tissue of the bone and *baste* the meat in marrowy goodness. Bones and meat don't work that way.

So now that I seem to have scienced all of the fun out of bone-in steaks, what is it that the bone does, and why do so many steak connoisseurs prefer a bone-in rib eye to a boneless one? Well, although meat science would tell us that based on palatability, a rib bone does not add flavor to the steak, this other science called psychology may be able to explain the difference in perceived eating satisfaction. Science—indeed, even meat science—tells us that our brains, when we observe or are told something specific, can make things taste different based on our perception. So maybe, indirectly, a bone-in steak, when viewed through the eyes of a hungry diner, does taste different from a boneless. It certainly looks cool! And (hashtag) coolness factor is definitely a real thing.

The rib eye, the main event of the rib primal, is also where we obtain the prime-rib roast. Unless, you have skipped around in this book and did not already read about beef grades, then what is about to be stated may not make much sense. Sorry to say this, but not all prime ribs are USDA Prime. The prime rib is a roast made from a large section of the rib primal. It's what would ultimately become rib eye steaks if you were to, in fact, cut steaks. It is almost always a pleasing eating experience, but the word *prime* in prime rib is merely a name assigned to it. It's not reflecting a USDA grade.

All cuts can come from all different grades of beef. A prime rib roast, more accurately considered a rib roast or rib eye roast, can come from a USDA Select, USDA Choice, or USDA Prime carcass. And technically, it can come from other carcasses that are assigned the lesser-known grade designations or no grade at all. Just remember that if one is searching for a specific eating experience at a certain value, don't let the term prime rib be confused with a precise USDA grade. Whew, meat from beef can be just as complicated as the processes that grow the animal.

The rib primal is also home to a specific type of short ribs. Short ribs can technically come from the chuck, the rib, or the plate beef carcass primals. However, probably some of the most exciting versions of this type of tasty cut will come from the rib. Because beef fabrication (again, beef butchery) has advanced over the years and some of the lines that designate one beef primal from the other have been a bit blurred, the rib primal short ribs can also be called the plate short ribs. But really, what we're talking about are some big, long-bone, barbeque-style short ribs.

These are the ones that I also often refer to as brontosaurus short ribs because of the massive rib bone that is associated with them. They look amazing, and they certainly taste great! Because they are so big (nearly twelve inches in length often) the term *short* rib is almost a bit off base. Sometimes, I joke and call them merely *shortened* ribs, *ha!* Anyway, the rib primal definitely packs a punch when it comes to cuts that are tasty, look good, and are well-known.

Plate. Since I've just mentioned the plate, let's investigate that primal a little further. I'm not entirely sure how it got its name, but if you look up a photo of one and have a creative imagination, one could see that it does have a flat, almost dinner-plate-like appearance. The plate is located around the base of the rib cage of the beef carcass and has a lot of tasty fat in it. Beyond the short ribs that share a common location with the rib primal, the plate also is where the skirt steaks are located.

Skirt steak, in the past, has been a lower-cost item for a lot of Latin American cuisine. However, more recently, the skirt steaks have definitely grown in popularity across many other cuisines and, as a result, grown in value as well. The skirt steak is the classic cut for carne asada or fajita meat. The outside skirt steak—scientifically, the diaphragm of the animal—is the more tender of the two skirt steaks. The inside skirt steak, a much larger abdominal muscle, is a bit lower cost but also needs a little more help due to being less tender, usually requiring a marinade of citric acid or something to help soften the bite a bit. Both are great on the grill and can also be used as stir-fry.

The plate also has some great use as a classic pastrami raw ingredient. In fact, in the beef packing world, the lowest part of the belly or navel of the plate is also sometimes called the *pastrami*. More contemporary pastrami is made from leaner cuts like the brisket or cuts from the round (hind leg), but a classic pastrami is fatty and rich and comes from the low part of the plate.

This is also a cut that is becoming popular for making beef bacon. Beef bacon has a whole new dimension of flavor that, sorry to say, pork has a hard time bringing to the table. Don't get me wrong. I love pork bacon, but once you've had beef bacon, you'll realize that it is a robust sensation that is most certainly a game changer.

The plate has some succulent items in it, but because of its limited size and dimension as well as its fattiness, it tends to get a bit less attention than some of the other cuts.

Loin. The beef loin is the primal with probably the highest dollar potential, although the rib primal definitely gives it a run for its money. The reason I say that the loin is a pricey proposition is because it contains some of the very well-known steak items and a few roasts that are starting to become quite popular as well. The loin is also pretty good size and contains some major subprimals such as the short loin and the sirloin. Let's dig in!

The highest-priced cut in the carcass on a per-pound basis is almost always going to be the tenderloin. The tenderloin is the most tender cut in the entire carcass and as a result is highly sought-after by both grocery stores and restaurants. The tenderloin actually traverses across the two big subprimals in the loin. When the short loin is cut, it will contain half of the tenderloin, while the other half goes with the sirloin (under traditional fabrication practices). If one cuts a short loin, then it will be pretty quickly observed that this is where the T-bone and porterhouse steaks will be cut from.

A very common question is, what is the difference between a T-bone and a porterhouse? Often, my reply would be that it all depends on what the definition is based on, whoever is purchasing it, but the technical description is actually dependent on the size of the tenderloin when the steak is cut. The tenderloin must be 1.25 inches wide at its widest spot to be considered a porterhouse steak by USDA's definition. However, let's be honest, that's pretty small. Most porterhouse steaks will have a much wider tenderloin than 1.25 inches, and that is more likely the norm.

Also, technically, all porterhouses are T-bones as they all have the distinct T-shaped bone from the lumbar vertebrae of the beef carcass. However, not all T-bones are porterhouse steaks due to the limitation of the tenderloin dimension. All muscles are tapered and the tenderloin is much smaller the closer you move toward the head of the animal.

The T-bone and porterhouse also are where the strip loin steak is located. This is one steak that has a multitude of names and is probably most often referred to as the New York strip steak. The strip loin is actually the same muscle as the rib eye, but because of the primal from which it is cut, it gets a new name. It's also sometimes referred to as a "top loin" steak, a *shell* steak, a Kansas City strip steak (when it's bone-in), and in some parts, it's referred to as a *sirloin* steak. Yet under most circumstances, the sirloin steak is something else in the loin, which will be described next.

As we travel more posterior on the beef carcass, we end up at the sirloin. Sirloin actually is a French term meaning "on top of" or "above" the loin. This is because we hang the beef carcass from the hind leg and as a result, the more posterior cuts are actually higher up or above the more anterior cuts. The sirloin is a value proposition. There are two main subprimals to the sirloin: the top sirloin and the bottom sirloin.

The top sirloin is where we can obtain some very classic steakhouse steaks. The center cut top sirloin steak, also called the baseball sirloin, is hefty and satisfying cut. It is a beef steak lover's steak and epitomizes the steak-eating experience. It may not be as tender as the tenderloin, and it may not be as rich in marbling as a rib eye, but something about the top sirloin center cut steak makes it still a highly desirable item that can best be described as simply *sirloiney*. The top sirloin is also home to the top sirloin cap. The top sirloin cap is also known by the fanciful name *coulotte* and is a staple in Brazilian-style steakhouses and Latin American cuisine, where it is known as the *picanha/picaña* (Portuguese/Spanish). In recent years, the popularity of the coulotte for roasts and steaks has almost surpassed that of the center cut top sirloin.

The bottom sirloin consists of three cuts: the ball tip, the tri-tip, and the sirloin flap. All three of these cuts are distinctly different from one another. However, they are all great cuts and have unique versatility. The ball tip, which is a portion of the quadriceps of the animal, is a lean and rather tender cut. The ball tip often is seen as a relatively inexpensive steak or roast but also will shred nicely when slow cooked or braised.

The sirloin flap looks a lot like a thick skirt steak. Indeed, the sirloin flap can be used in a variety of applications similar to that of the skirt steak, but because of the added thickness, it can be used for other culinary applications as well. The sirloin flap has long been a staple in the New England region of the US, where it is merchandised as steak tips and often served with a sauce of sorts. A bit farther north, the sirloin flap is the go-to cut for French-speaking Canada, where it is served as a steak known as the bavette, a tasty and distinctive-textured cut that is very desirable and is finding a lot of value for a traditionally lower-cost area of the carcass.

The tri-tip is a cut that deserves a bit of pause and reflection. It is a cut that traditionally has been a very regional item, nearly unknown to the rest of the country. Its name is about as descriptive as can be of the cut. It is a very traditional grilling and direct-heat-barbecue cut of California and, until recently, has been one that was almost entirely eaten in that part of the country. However, with the migration of Californians from the state, so goes the culinary tradition, which meant that the tri-tip cut has been popping up all over the United States as a great cut for a variety of applications. The roast itself is of good value and is relatively easy to prepare. It is also one that regularly has a good amount of marbling, which lends itself to a richer flavor and, therefore, makes a pretty good grilling steak. The popularity of the tri-tip is to California what the brisket is to Texas. Interesting how the two former republics carry such a lofty beef-flavored tradition. Somewhat similar in some respects, yet very unique in others, just like the states themselves.

Flank. What do you get from the flank? Flank steak. Creative, huh? The flank steak has traditionally been a braised item and formerly thought of as a less-tender cut. However, if marinated in an acid such as lime juice, grilled, and then sliced thinly, it can be surprisingly tender. The flank steak is a rather lean cut, and the Italian tradition has used this as the main meat in braciola (braised flank steak). Although the flank steak is a great cut in its own right and has gained tremendous popularity, the flank primal actually has one other cut found in it.

Cattle, because of the way that nature made them, can't really reach their flank area if they have an itch. Thankfully, there's a thin muscle that we often simply call the "fly-twitch muscle" in the flank area that can help to send those little nuisances flying and provide relief for cattle without having to access that hard-to-reach area under the belly near the hind leg. When cattle are harvested, that thin muscle is mostly made into ground beef. However, it is a cut that can also be treated like a flank steak and is a popular cut in Argentinian cuisine called the *matambre*. The *matambre*, etymologically speaking, almost quite literally translates to "hunger killer," and when prepared in a slow-cooked or braised method, it will certainly live up to its rugged description.

Round. The hind leg of the beef is called the round. Why? Well, I believe it is because meatcutters don't have time to come up with superlative names, and like the flank, it was called what it is—round. Although the round resembles a supersized chicken drumstick, it has its circumference that definitely lives up to its name. The round is a large primal and, therefore, contains a lot of meat representing over twenty percent of the weight of the carcass. Very classic roasts are found in the round as well as a few value-oriented steaks.

The round is comprised of five main subprimals: top round, bottom round, eye of round, knuckle, and heel. Several of these subprimals are named as a result of their position on the animal or how they have been fabricated in the past. The top round and bottom round received their names because historically, butchers and meatcutters would lay the round primal on a table or cutting block, and the top round, which contains a portion of the pelvic bone, would be one of the first things removed from the round. The pelvic bone is located immediately adjacent to the inner thigh of the animal, which is also the top round proper. Thus, the top round was simply on top as the primal lies on the table, while the bottom round lies on the bottom. Alternative names to these cuts, as I've alluded to already based on their anatomical location on the animal, would be inside round (top) and outside round (bottom), which quite literally is the description of the thigh locations (inner thigh = inside round = top round; outer thigh = outside round = bottom round).

The eye of round lies between the top round and the bottom round, and when connected to the bottom round itself then, that combination is called a *gooseneck* (this is an instance where we wonder what folks were thinking when this cut was named…oh well). The eye of round is essentially the hamstring of the beef carcass. As a result, it indeed has a lot of connective tissue (chewy stuff) interwoven in the muscle, which leads to a bit of tenderness challenges.

Amazingly, the eye of round also is one of the most popularly purchased cuts from the round, most likely due to the fact that when steaks are cut from it, they are nearly perfect circles and look really nice in a meat case. This is a bit deceiving. Although the cut is very affordable, has an appealingly lean and symmetrically circular appearance, this cut is probably one of the toughest cuts in the entire carcass. What that means is I highly recommend that you *do not grill this steak!* All beef is great. Just some are better than others for certain applications. The eye of round can make a nice lean carving roast or can be slow cooked to help tenderize it a bit, but as a grilling steak, nearly all meat scientists would advise against this practice. You have been warned.

The knuckle is the predominant portion of the quadriceps, the minor section of which remains on the loin as the ball tip when the round is separated from the loin. Meat scientists have actually identified some rather tender cuts in the knuckle. However, it takes a bit of knife work to get to those tender cuts, and as a result, the knuckle is often simply roasted, cut into inexpensive steaks, or used as a main component in ground sirloin. Sirloin? Wait (you say)! I thought we were talking about beef round, not the sirloin (you think to yourself). Well (I say), this is indeed true, but with just about everything in life, there are exceptions and situations of "it depends." The knuckle's alternate name is actually the "sirloin tip." This is not a mistake as it sits just adjacent to the sirloin on the beef carcass and, depending on how the carcass is cut, could actually have been left on the sirloin portion of the loin in some cases.[5]

---

[5] Most beef carcasses in the United States, contemporarily, are cut using what would be considered the *Chicago* break. This is a straight cut with a bone saw to separate the beef round from the beef loin at the hip and femur joint. The Chicago break will cut the quadriceps of the carcass into two pieces: the ball tip (loin) and the knuckle (round). This is a practice that has a deep root in the development of the United States and the boom of the middle class in the late 1800s and early 1900s.

It is very well known that as a nation develops economically, the populace demands and introduces more meat into their diet. At

Beef aging

After all of that effort to raise the animal, harvest the beef, and cut up the carcass, there's still work to be done.

---

the turn of the twentieth century, Chicago, Illinois, was the butcher to the world. During this period of rapid industrial expansion and economic prosperity—and therefore, the demand for meat—the meat-packing companies in Chicago developed more rapid and industrialized means of cutting carcasses to more efficiently get meat on the table of Americans and beyond. A very efficient means of doing so would be to limit the precision fabrication styles of the butcher trades prior to this time, which would isolate individual muscles that are variable in shape and, therefore, at the time, were challenging to cut out of the carcass mechanically. However, there were big saws that could make big efficient cuts, resulting in more throughput and more meat getting out to the masses.

There are classically three different styles of fabricating the beef round from the beef loin: the Chicago break, the New York-style break, and the Diamond Cut. The Chicago break is what was just described. The Diamond Cut would actually leave more meat on the round at the quadriceps, but while making essentially a diamond point on the sirloin section of the loin, this would cut through the tri-tip and sirloin flap effectively ruining those cuts (thankfully, we don't practice this any longer). The Diamond Cut loin would be a more trim loin that could be more easily fabricated into steaks back when butchers in metropolitan areas bought whole loins and did not know about the value of the bottom sirloin cuts.

The remaining round-loin separation style therefore is the New York-style break. The New York-style break would actually separate the quadriceps from the hind leg prior to separating the rest of the hind leg (the round) from the loin. This additional bit of quadriceps on the bottom sirloin after the round was removed would be a point or *tip* of the bottom sirloin. Therefore, the New York-style round-loin separation would produce a sirloin *tip*, which is why the quadriceps of the carcass uses the term "sirloin tip" sometimes when referencing the beef knuckle. Fascinating!

Beef is certainly scrumptious on its own, but there is a common practice that is utilized to enhance the already delectable protein: aging.

Under most circumstances, beef is aged on its way to the final point of sale, be it grocery store or restaurant. In industrialized nations, such as the United States, the overwhelming majority of fresh beef is packaged into vacuum packaging. This style of packaging helps to maintain the moisture and yield of the meat while providing a synthetic protective barrier for protection against the outside environment. Meat in vacuum package and stored in refrigeration is known as "wet aged." Wet aging simply means that the meat is not allowed to have evaporative loss of moisture, which was actually quite common prior to the 1970s when vacuum packaging became mainstream in the beef business. Aging meat allows for natural enzymes in the meat to break down the muscle fibers over time, which enhances the tenderness of the final product. Wet aging is by far the most common means of aging meat, especially beef. However, in recent years, "dry aging" has made a resurgence among beef meat enthusiasts.

Dry aging is simply storing meat under refrigeration without any packaging, which allows for natural moisture loss to occur. Because of this natural evaporative loss of moisture over time, the innate flavors in the meat are concentrated, similar to if one were to make a reduction sauce. The flavors are then more pronounced and enhanced when compared with traditional wet-aged beef. Because of the lack of packaging, dry-aged beef also will often have mold growth of some type on the outer surface of the cuts being aged, which have been shown to impart their own unique flavors as well. Dry-aged beef is often described as having a browned, roasted, robust beef flavor and is frequently accompanied by additional flavors such as earthy, nutty, oaky, and cheesy. The subsequent flavors are likely a result of the unique molds found on dry-aged beef that are usually specific to the location in which the beef is being aged.

Wet-aging beef is super simple and extremely consistent and repeatable, which is why it is probably one of the most popular means of aging beef. However, due to the nature of the anaerobic environment in the vacuum package where beef is being wet aged, there is often going to be some sour flavor notes developed in beef aged in this manner for an extended period of time (generally greater than thirty-five days). As much as we do our best in the meat business to maintain cleanliness and an aseptic environment, meat in a packing plant is not necessarily sterile. This means that there are still microbes that make their way onto meat and into the packaging at some time. These microbes are not pathogenic (food illness organisms). However, they are most often a very common bacteria that is native to just about every environment in which humans exist: lactic acid-producing bacteria.

Lactic acid has been mentioned during the fermentation of feed by ruminant animals, and it is yet again present when food is stored under anaerobic conditions, including meat. Lactic acid bacteria can still survive in vacuum packaging where no oxygen is present, but as a result of their survival, they produce lactic acid as a byproduct, which will produce a slight sour flavor when tasted. Lactic acid bacteria are the ones responsible for the tangy flavor of yogurt and some of the tartness found in sauerkraut. In very well-aged beef, there will also be a hint of sourness to the taste. This isn't a good thing or a bad thing. As I say, it's just a thing. Most folks don't even notice the slight sourness of wet aged beef quite possibly because it is almost expected. It's the flavor that folks have become so accustomed to with beef found in nearly every supermarket and steakhouse, and therefore, it's not noticed. What is noticed is when the sourness is *not* there.

Dry-aged beef, as mentioned, brings about a robust accompaniment of flavors that wet aged does not necessarily contribute. As mentioned earlier, microbes are thought to play a part in this distinct delivery of tastes. However, lactic acid-producing bacteria are not among those microbes that contribute much to the dry-aged-beef flavor. In fact, science has shown that bacteria actually have a hard time surviving the drier surface of dry-aged beef due to the evaporation of surface moisture. Molds and yeasts are really the ones that can survive these conditions. Therefore, when many folks eat dry-aged beef, they say they notice a sweetness to the meat. What they are more likely noticing is the *lack* of lactic acid, which makes it taste less sour than normally expected. This, too, helps to differentiate the flavors of wet-aged versus dry-aged beef.

Because of the extremely consistent *environment* in which wet-aged beef resides, it is very similar in taste every single time (if marbling were equal among steaks, of course). Dry-aged beef, however, is much more of an art than a science. Dry-aging cooler conditions will vary with regard to humidity, airflow, and even the native molds and yeasts in the air of the building in which the cooler is located.[6]

Cooler conditions for wet aging beef is similar to dry aging with regard to temperature. Good aging of beef occurs around thirty-six degrees Fahrenheit. This is cold enough to stay below the "danger zone" (above forty degrees Fahrenheit, temperature where foodborne-illness organisms grow well) but not too cold where the meat begins to freeze (twenty-eight degrees Fahrenheit). However, similarities between wet-aging and dry-aging environmental controls pretty much end at temperature. Because dry aging is at the mercy of the flow of air and ambient humidity in coolers, there can be a lot of variation in this type of beef product. Yet I think that is what gives dry-aged beef its charm and character compared to wet-aged beef.[7]

---

[6] Yes, molds, yeast, and bacteria are all floating around in the air pretty much at all times. They are also on our hands, surfaces, and most food, especially prior to cooking. This is not to sound alarming. It's to remind the reader that we live with microorganisms all the time and that we coexist with those lifeforms just fine. There certainly are pathogenic microorganisms that can indeed make us sick, but compared to all of the others that we encounter, those illness bugs are actually few and far between. Thank goodness! In fact, we regularly use microorganisms to help us with making food such as yogurt, bread, beer, soy sauce, and certain types of sausages. It is always important to be conscious of those microbes, but we don't necessarily need to fear them. Simply be aware.

[7] It may come as a surprise to a lot of folks, but meat freezes at twenty-eight degrees Fahrenheit, not the commonly thought of thirty-two degrees Fahrenheit, which is the freezing point of water. Although meat does contain a lot of water, there's also a lot of other things diluted in that cellular water in meat and muscle that lower the freezing temperature. Also, the more fat there is in meat, the lower the freezing temperature will be. Freezing is a great way to preserve the quality of meats, but it needs to be done in a way that no meat surface is exposed to air,

All said, however, dry-aging beef comes at a cost. Constant cooler management, product rotation, airflow monitoring, evaporative moisture loss, and mold growth that ultimately has to be cut away prior to cutting the final steaks add to the expense but also value of dry-aged beef. It's not for everyone, but dry-aged beef definitely has its following. I know I enjoy it!

Beef meat science is a vast and expansive discipline that has many minds working to constantly improve the taste and safety of the end product. It's also a superdynamic and rewarding arena combining food science with animal science. What a pair.

---

which will lead to what is known as freezer burn. Tight-fitting vacuum packaging is the best way to freeze meat.

CHAPTER 6

It's Not a Cow—It's a Mother

Cattle are from the taxonomical scientific designation within the kingdom Animalia (a complex amalgamation of eukaryotic cells that utilize oxygen and can move), phylum Chordata (has a vertebral column and a spinal cord), and class Mammalia (they produce milk for their young—mammals). Nature is fascinating, and milk is one of those truly fascinating materials generated naturally by mammals.

When one spends significant time with animals, you really begin to appreciate the different types of complex creatures within the animal kingdom. You have the superbasic sponges that are about as simple of an animal as they can come. You have worms, where we begin to see some of the most basic of circulatory systems. Arthropods, animals with an exoskeleton (skeletal structure on the outside of their body), bring in a new level of complexity and otherworldliness (e.g., spiders, insects, and crustaceans). Fish, reptiles, and amphibians show us just how much more can be accomplished with a higher-functioning circulatory and more advanced nervous systems. Birds bring yet another layer of intricacy in their ability to maintain their own body temperature and have very specialized features that are adaptable to a variety of environments. But the animals that have truly shown what a multifaceted and highly intricate natural arrangement of tissues and organs can bring to the world are the mammals.

We humans (in case we need to be reminded) are mammals. The females of our species have the ability to nurse our young. Almost magically, the components in the life-giving substance known as milk can take a human neonate from around seven pounds to nearly three times that size within a year of life providing little other than just that, milk. Granted, this is a gross overgeneralization of child rearing but the point being that milk is that amazing component that mammals have at their disposal to help grow and nurture their young in a way that other animals really can't.

But this is a book about cattle, not child development (however, in my family, both go somewhat hand-in-hand). Although humans are mammals, the females of the species really generate milk for only the very early development of babies. Yet somewhere along the lines of human progress, people have observed the amazing nutritive benefits of milk and have sought other sources of milk, which could be a source of food for people of all ages. Goats and sheep were likely some of the earliest of animals used in agriculture for producing milk for human consumption, but once cattle came into the playbook of animal-sourced food production, the game really changed.

As mentioned earlier, cattle, at birth, are often weighing over eighty pounds. Because of their size, they are in need of a large volume of nutrients to not only survive but also grow. Milk is able to provide all that the growing baby (human, cattle, etc.) needs to thrive. There are six main nutrients that nutritionists discuss: water, carbohydrates (sugars), lipids (fats), protein, vitamins, and minerals. If one were to look into the makeup of milk, it contains all of these things, and in incredibly ideal amounts, for the baby of the species in question. Although cow's milk is not exactly the same as human, it still contains great amounts of what is needed for the human body to thrive. Also, because of their size, cattle are able to provide a lot of milk compared to goats and sheep. It's probably the reason why so much milk and dairy products are produced from cattle compared to all of the other domesticated livestock species.

Making milk

As mentioned before, milk is produced for young to consume and grow, but prior to the young's being in existence, the physiology of reproduction needs to be initiated (wow, did I take all the fun out of that or what!). At late gestation (pregnancy), milk formation will begin to be initiated in the mammary gland of the pregnant female. All of the components needed to make milk are going to be delivered in the bloodstream, but it is the unique cells in the mammary tissue that are able to take the basic building blocks of circulating nutrients and compose them into what is later observed as milk.

In a dairy cow, it is estimated that it takes about four hundred gallons of blood circulation to produce one gallon of milk. Considering each cow can produce about ten gallons of milk a day on average, that's a very robust circulatory system!

Now, if you've been following along closely, you're already familiar with how amazing ruminant animals are. They can take indigestible plant material, ferment it, and turn it into nutrients that their bodies can use. When the body of the milk cow is needing to produce milk, there are certainly considerations that are required to make sure that the cow is able to produce to her full potential. Once again, careful consideration is made with the formulation of nutrients for the feed that the milk cow will consume. Although there are certainly pasture-run dairy farms in North America, the reality is that because of the seasonality of farming—and thus, pasture availability—in order to have abundant milk year-round, farmers in most developed countries either supplement their cows with mixed stored feed (similar in some respects to what is fed to beef cattle but far more roughages), or they provide the feed mixture entirely as a means of best utilizing the land and feed resources around the dairy farm.

The mammary gland in a milk cow is called an udder. Cattle have four compartments to their udder (as opposed to goats and sheep that have only two), which helps in the tremendous volume of milk that they are able to generate. Inside the mammary gland is a vast network of blood vessels that surround tiny little pockets in the udder called *alveoli*. These alveoli are lined with the specialized cells that are able to take the nutrients in the blood and convert those basic nutrients into the more unique nutrients found in milk.

Water. Water is the primary media in which the nutrients of milk will be suspended. It's also one of the most important nutrients for life. Living organisms cannot survive long without sufficient quantities of water, especially young growing babies, and as such, the milk cow provides a lot of water in the milk she produces. Water helps to transport the other nutrients in milk, but it also provides a source of water to the animal consuming it (i.e., baby cattle, people, etc.). Water is the largest component of what mammals are made of, and as a result, we'll see a lot of water in milk. But water is only part of the equation.

Carbohydrates. The main type of carbohydrate found in milk is the sugar called lactose. Lactose is going to provide the immediate energy that the growing baby will need to thrive and function as it is a source of glucose. Glucose is a very important simple sugar that provides readily accessible energy for the body.

Unfortunately, lactose is often the reason why there are intolerances to milk and dairy products for people who cannot digest this carbohydrate fully—lactose intolerance. In order to overcome this challenge of lactose intolerance, we have been able to introduce enzymes that can be taken orally prior to consuming dairy products that can break down lactose and make it so a person does not have to suffer the consequences of indigestion if indeed they are lactose intolerant. Furthermore, dairy processors have been more and more increasingly able to *preconvert* the lactose in milk so that it can be consumed by those who want to enjoy dairy but are intolerant to the lactose in it.

Lactose is not just found in cow's milk but in all milk from all mammalian species. As the name implies, it quite literally is the sugar formed during *lactation*, the production of milk.

Lipids/fat. Milk fat in cow's milk is often referred to as *butterfat* or *cream*. It is suspended in the watery solution, but because fat and water do not mix, it will eventually separate out of the watery portion. This is the same reaction with an oil-and-vinegar salad dressing. Lipids/fats are less dense than water. They are also what is called hydrophobic (literally meaning afraid of water), which means that chemically speaking, they will not mix naturally with water. Therefore, most milk purchased in a grocery store will have the term *homogenized* on the label. Homogenization is a step at the creamery (milk-processing facility), where the milk is forced through tiny holes that break up the milk fat into droplets that will therefore suspend in the watery portion of the milk and not separate out. Otherwise, as the axiom states, the cream will rise to the top.

Cow's milk is naturally around four percent fat. The amount of fat found in milk at a grocery store will be adjusted in a creamery where, because of the natural tendency of milk fat to separate from the watery portion, a centrifuge machine is used to spin the milk—prior to homogenization, of course—and the lighter cream will be separated from the watery portion quite easily and effectively. The cream can be used for making butter, ice cream, etc. or mixed back in with the *skimmed* milk to a proportion, which is desired for the end user. What is considered "whole milk" is actually milk that contains almost exactly 3.25 percent milk fat, unless otherwise noted on the label. This is often a misunderstood concept as whole milk is nearly ninety-seven percent fat-free. The little increments of decreased fat percentage really should be looked at as a difference in flavor, not necessarily a big difference in dietary fat consumption for those who enjoy a glass of milk from time to time.

Milk fat is highly variable in percentage of the milk, depending on which breed of cow it is produced from. Generally, milk fat will be near four percent, but some breeds of dairy cows will have higher percentages of milk fat, while some will have lower. The Jersey breed of cattle (relatively small with solid-brown hair coloring) tends to lead in the percentage of milk fat in their milk. Jerseys have been often associated as the breed that is great for making high-fat cheeses, butter, and ice cream because of their tendency to have that higher fat percentage in their milk.

However, because of their size, they don't have the capacity to produce nearly as much milk as the typical Holstein. When people think of a milk cow, they most likely think of the Holstein, which is the larger breed with random black-and-white hair patterns. Holstein cattle are known to produce the largest volume of milk per animal. However, this also comes with a decrease in milk fat percentage. Because of their ability to convert feed nutrients into milk volume, Holstein cattle have become by far the leading breed of cattle with regard to milk production.

Over the years, fat consumption in the diet of humans has received a bad reputation and has been considered something to avoid. However, more recent understandings of nutrients in a human diet has demonstrated how fat—yes, indeed, even milk fat—is beneficial and can be a healthy part of a balanced diet.

Protein. There are different types of proteins found in milk, and milk is a great source of protein in a person's diet. Depending on the time of lactation (period of a mammal's life when milk is being produced), the protein components will change. We've discussed colostrum (milk generated at the first twenty-four to forty-eight hours after giving birth), which is a rather thick and yellowish-colored milk that the cow makes. The really special part of colostrum is actually the protein components in it. Many of the proteins are antibodies that help to kick-start the calf's immune system. But this milk protein makeup changes very quickly because nature made it so the calf can really only absorb these proteins within the first twenty-four hours of life anyway. Therefore, the cow doesn't need to produce these specialized proteins in the milk and adjusts the milk manufacturing process to more of a means for food utilization—good for the calf and good for the people who enjoy dairy products!

After that initial time period of twenty-four to forty-eight hours, the largest percentage of protein found in milk will be one called casein. Casein makes up about eighty percent of the proteins found in milk and is the most important one for making cheese. Casein is coagulated in the stomach of the calf by the stomach acids as well as by an enzyme called rennet. When cheese is made, people at a creamery will simply mimic what is happening in the stomach of the young animal and either apply a weak acid, enzyme (natural or manufactured), or both to allow for the casein protein to coagulate and bind together to make the cheese. This also will separate the casein from the whey protein (the remaining twenty percent of the milk protein).

Casein and whey proteins are the allergens that some people are allergic to in milk. These proteins are found in pretty much all milk types, but there are certain versions of these proteins that cause a reaction. There are now cows being raised that produce a version of casein that is nonreactive to those who have milk allergies, making milk something that can be back in their diets. *Yay!*

Vitamins. Vitamins are naturally occurring chemicals in bodies and in foods that are needed for regular body functions. They are going to often be more complex than minerals but have similar mechanisms. Milk is a naturally great source of several B vitamins, including the big one, B12. Vitamin B12 is really only naturally sourced from animal proteins (meat, milk, and eggs) and is absolutely essential for proper body functions, especially within the nervous system and for development of red blood cells. Milk also is a natural source of Vitamin A, which is important for good eyesight. Vitamin D is often added in milk as a fortifying vitamin to encourage good bone growth. Vitamin D actually helps the body absorb calcium, a mineral that is in high quantities in milk!

Minerals. Speaking of minerals, especially calcium, milk is that magical food that packs what is needed to grow and maintain a body. Calcium in a growing animal or human is really important in the diet to help with those bones that are trying to grow. But calcium actually has a second task in milk. Remember how I mentioned that the protein casein in milk is negatively charged? Well, since nature likes balance, the calcium, a positively charged ion, in milk helps to balance the negative chemical charge of casein and thereby creating that balance that nature likes to have. *Wow!* What an amazing feat. Great job nature!

Collecting the milk at the farm

When those alveoli in the udders of the cow are full with their nutritious and tasty treat (milk), the udder will look like a rather full bag. In fact, that's what the udder is often referred to by most dairy farmers, *bags*—rather insensitive, huh? Under the circumstances where there is a nursing calf, the sounds of the calf or the stimulation of the teats by the nursing calf will send a signal to the brain of the cow, which will, in turn, release a hormone called oxytocin into the bloodstream. Oxytocin is what allows for milk *letdown* and actually causes muscle in the udder to squeeze the alveoli in the udder, which helps to push the milk out and into the mouth of the awaiting calf.

Yet a big reality of dairy farming is that milk cows have now been selectively bred so well for milk production that one calf would never be able to drink all of the milk that a commercial milk cow could produce. Again, let's be reminded that these are not the same cattle that are used specifically for beef (Angus, Hereford, Charolais, etc.). These are cattle that have been specially bred over several hundred years for milk production (Holstein, Jersey, Guernsey, Brown Swiss, and Ayrshire). This focus on making milk has led to the need to have a lot more hands-on (literally) approach with the calf of the modern milk cow.[8]

Calves born on a dairy farm will be hand-raised by farmers using bottles to provide milk necessary for the calf to grow well. Most of the milk that calves receive on a dairy farm is actually going to come from milk collected there on the farm. There are instances when a cow that is in production that may need to be administered a bit of medicine for one reason or another. The milk from that cow that has received medicine cannot go into the human food supply for several days, but it can be fed to the growing calves on the dairy farm.

Milk cows, because of their incredible potential to produce milk, are grateful to be milked by the dairy farmers. Anyone who has spent time with milk cows can see the interest and desire to be milked when the udder is full as it is believed that a very full udder can sometimes be a little uncomfortable for the cow, thereby making it important for the dairy farmer to milk the cow on a regular basis.

---

[8] Calves at a dairy farm are raised apart from their mothers early on in life, generally within the first twenty-four hours of life. Dairy calves will be raised in small hutches either independently or in small groups to allow for good nutritional and health management by the dairy farmers. Although milk cows do have a lot of ability to generate a lot of milk, they don't necessarily seem to miss their calves. The calves grow up being very tame and are accustomed to people being around, which makes them quite safe when they are older and much larger. The female calves on a dairy farm will be raised to become milkers in the herd later in life, while most of the male calves will be raised up for beef.

Most milk cows will be milked twice a day. However, some will be milked three times a day.

Milk cows really like routine. Heck, most any animal really appreciates the predictability and consistency of a good routine (I know I do). Spending time on a dairy one will quickly realize just how predictable a milk cow can be and how much they, too, appreciate that predictability. Milk cows can be so committed to a routine that some will arrive in a specific order in the milk barn and prefer a specific spot in the parlor (another name for the milking barn) at a specific time in the day. Of course, how different is this from us humans who like to have our special coffee meetup at the same place, with the same friends, sitting at the same table at a similar time each day/week? When you think of it, routine is important to both animals and humans, and in the dairy farming community, timing is certainly considered with regard to maintaining a content herd.

When it's time to milk the cows, farmers will either rouse the cows from their barn or pasture and lead them up to the milking barn. Amazingly, this is actually the beginning of the milk letdown process. I've seen where the simple auditory stimuli of a clanging chain on a gate (the same gate each day, mind you) is enough of a stimulation in the brain to cause the oxytocin to be released into the bloodstream of the cow and bring about the milk letdown process. Incredible how tied the body is to the external stimuli that can elicit a response as specific as the squeezing of the alveoli in the udder.

When the cow arrives at the milk parlor, the farmer will gently wash the udder of any visible dirt or possible contaminants and dry the teat with a clean paper towel. This will also be the time for the farmer to do what is called *priming* the teat. Priming is just like the motion of hand milking a cow where the teat is squeezed by hand to bring about a little flow of milk. Priming the teat is very similar to the action felt by a nursing calf and is yet another external stimulus that tells the brain of the cow that it's time to let the milk flow.

Milking machines are used by nearly all commercial dairy farms, large and small. Milk machines are simply four tubes, called "teat cups," with rubber hoses that connect to a central canister all linked to a vacuum machine. The vacuum machine has a pulsing action that also stimulates the feel of a nursing calf while the vacuum itself is used to collect the milk through a system of stainless steel pipes into what is called a bulk tank. The bulk tank is where the milk from all of the other cows is stored until it is ready to be transported by a milk truck, which is a large truck with a tank on the back of it up to something the size of a tractor trailer with very large tanks. Most folks may have seen these types of trucks on the road, and they are very similar in build to most other tanker trucks that transport liquids.

Once the cow is done milking and the flow of milk becomes minimal, the dairy farmer will turn off a valve on the milking machine connected to the cow, which cuts off the vacuum, and the teat cups release from the teats on the udder. The teats are then dipped in an iodine or antimicrobial solution that helps to keep the teats clean and prevent any pathogens from entering the teat opening. This is important to keep the teats from becoming infected, which can be very painful to the cow. After the teats are dipped, the cow is sent back to their respective barn or pasture to eat, socialize, and await the next milking.

This entire process is becoming more and more mechanized to where there are giant parlors that actually rotate like a merry-go-round (they are actually called carousel parlors), which allow for a continuous, albeit very slow, movement of the cows getting milked. The cows don't seem to mind the ride, and it creates a very efficient flow of milk cows into and out of the barn. We're even beginning to see fully automated milking robotics on the dairy farm that makes it so when the cow feels like it, she can be milked as many times as she likes during the day. However, what we're still seeing is that naturally twice a day is still quite common.

Milk at the creamery

Milk-processing facilities, or creameries, are fascinating pieces of human engineering as well as a plumber's nightmare. Anyone who tours a creamery will be impressed by the immense amount of stainless steel piping in the building. This is because stainless steel is very resistant to rust and is durable enough to withstand the cleaning agents (i.e., soaps, detergents, etc.) necessary to keep the milk equipment very sanitary.

We've already mentioned how milk is transported to the creamery, how it undergoes separation to divorce the cream from the skim milk, but much more can happen at a creamery to ensure that milk is safe and tasty. Upon arrival at the creamery, all milk are sampled from the truck to look at components (fat, protein, etc.), which are important for the premiums that dairy farmers can be paid. Fat and protein in milk are highly valuable, and so it's important that if a dairy farmer has a herd that can produce high cream and protein content that they are rewarded financially for it.

Other things that milk is sampled for are antibiotics. The reality is that sometimes cattle get sick, and it's the farmer and rancher's obligation to take care of the health of the animal. Antibiotics are helpful to cure an animal of a bacterial illness, but they are not allowed to be in food for human consumption. That's why all milk is tested to make sure there are no antibiotics in it.

Once the milk is sampled and confirmed that it is safe to use for food, it enters the creamery system, where it will be separated into known amounts of milk fat and skim milk, and if it is destined to be traditionally bottled fluid milk, it will be homogenized so that the cream content does not separate from the skim milk.

A process that nearly all milk goes through, and for good reason, is something called pasteurization. Pasteurization is a heat treatment of the milk that is used to kill off pathogenic organisms that could make us sick. Pasteurization is named after the French scientist Louis Pasteur, who developed pasteurization back in the mid-1800s as a means of stabilizing wine without sacrificing the quality of it. This process has been adapted and adopted by the dairy community to ensure the same nutrient content of the milk, but by killing potentially harmful bacteria that may make their way into the milk at the dairy farm. Let's remember, we're still dealing with animals, and as much as the dairy farmer tries to keep the animal clean, we still need to be conscious of the possibility of something that could be on the teat that could make us sick. Therefore, to keep those enjoying dairy products safe, we wash the teat, we dry the teat, we dip the teat, but we also pasteurize the milk as yet an additional precaution to keep things safe.

Contrary to some people's belief, pasteurization does not change the nutrient content of the milk. Okay, actually, it does. It reduces the amount of Vitamin C in the milk. But let's be honest. Milk has an inconsequential amount of Vitamin C to begin with. Trying to use milk as a dietary source of Vitamin C is like trying to use a potato chip as a source for drinking water. There's a chance there's some water in it, but it's inconsequential. What pasteurization does is that it makes milk and dairy products reliably safe to consume without the fear of encountering a food borne illness. Pasteurization doesn't necessarily sterilize, but it does help extend the shelf life of milk and make it super safe.

Although many folks don't enjoy a glass of milk every morning as was often done in the past, dairy products have still found their way into our lives, and I'm thankful for that. Kids can still greatly benefit from the healthy nutrients provided by milk while delighting in a yogurt as a morning snack. Cheese comes in an unbelievable amounts of forms and styles, and each delivers with it not only nutrients but delight in flavor, texture, and style. Butter is back on the table, which makes me certainly happy. It turns out that the natural fatty spreadable pleasure that is butter is not as bad as it was made out to be back in the late twentieth century, another example of really investigating something before condemning it.

Milk and milk products have been a part of civilization for a really long time. I, for one, am grateful for the tasty way that nature has delivered nutrients for our survival, and I'm grateful for the cattle and dairy producers who help make it happen!

CHAPTER 7

It's Not a Cow—It's a Dependent

Folks who have had the pleasure of working with cattle know that they become somewhat a part of the family. Along with this comes many experiences that parallel family dynamics, and as such, it means that cattle are reliant upon us for their well-being as we are for their ability to produce meat and milk. If this book has inspired you to jump right out there and become a proud owner of your very own bovine, here're a few more things to consider: health, weather, and production practices.

Cattle health

Like all animals, there's always going to be the chance for illness to occur. Illnesses are one of those unavoidable manifestations with living things, a consequence of living, I suppose. Thankfully, our livestock have rather robust immune systems and are well adapted to a variety of environments, but there's always the chance for cattle to become sick. That's why, you'll find, that most cattle producers are not only part nutritionist, part reproductive physiologist, part endocrinologist, part truck driver, and part farmer, but they're also part veterinarian.

I must, at this point, make it perfectly clear that the veterinary profession is a very noble career and one that takes a tremendous amount of dedication and time to achieve the degree. But I will also grant that folks who raise cattle for a living have a very good working relationship with their veterinarian and, as a result, will often learn a thing or two along the way to help them in the day-to-day care of their critters.

Difficult health situations cattle may encounter could begin at birth. There are over thirty million calves born in the United States every year. With those numbers, you're bound to encounter a tough birth or two. People who grow up around cattle learn early on where babies come from and what can go wrong if nature doesn't play exactly by the rules. I recall at a young age helping my dad late at night on the business end of a cow that happened to be having trouble giving birth. Now, mind you, my dad is a carpenter, not a veterinarian, but he also grew up around cattle and had picked up the know-how on what to do when a calf is having trouble being born.

Challenging births are similar in just about all animals, it may be due to poor positioning of the calf in the birth canal, or simply too big of a calf for what the momma was meant to handle. The poor-presentation part is one that can be a bit complicated but not impossible. Sometimes, it's as simple as readjusting a leg so that it is able to more easily slide out of the birth canal, but there are times when the calf is simply turned around or upside-down in the uterus of the cow. In either case, the rancher will need to use their best imagination as to what they feel the calf is up to and help to reposition the calf so that it is able to be born correctly.

The too-big-calf dilemma is another story. This can happen when the bun spends a little too much time in the oven, but it is more likely due to the genetics of the sire and dam, and the birth weight of the calf is simply really big. In these cases, it's imperative that the calf and cow are helped by the rancher, and it's usually via the help of strong arms and a little bit of leverage. Yes, in the calves that seem to be too big for the momma to bring to the light, we grab the front legs of the calf and help that momma when she pushes. It's literally called *pulling* the calf.

Thankfully, big calves are becoming less and less frequent in the cattle world. This is because we are getting better at identifying bulls that can be bred to cows, which, in turn, have calves that are smaller but still are able to grow well later on in life. If the calf is small enough for a cow to give birth on their own, that is a very good thing that cattle ranchers definitely value.

Now, once the calf is born and has had its fill of the antibody-packed colostrum from its mother, it's usually on a great path for success. But that's not the end of health management of cattle. They are still susceptible to disease, and as a result, cattle ranchers are diligent about preventing illness at every level of the production phase. This is where the adage "an ounce of prevention is worth a pound of cure" really comes into play.

The way that illnesses are first prevented is simply by good cattle management. Keeping them content, calm, and minimizing stresses will limit the chances of contracting diseases. Think about the last time you got sick. Were you anxious, eating poorly, or all around agitated? It's the same with cattle. However, even the best of management programs still have to contend with pathogens from time to time. This is why cattle ranchers are also diligent about vaccinations. Sometimes, the term vaccination is thrown around loosely in the animal and human health world, and I've found that many folks don't understand that vaccinations are very different from antibiotics, so let's explain these, shall we?

A vaccine is something given to the animal to prevent the disease. Vaccines are usually a disabled version of the virus or bacteria in question or a killed version of the virus or bacteria from which we're trying to prevent the animal of becoming sick. Vaccines are important to be given early on in an animal's life and subsequently as needed to prevent a disease from occurring. Vaccines are usually very low doses and are very affordable compared to treatments of the disease later on. Vaccines teach the body what to look for with regard to the disease-causing agent (bacteria or viruses), which builds up antibodies for that illness and protects the animal in case they do come in contact with an infected herd mate.

Many of the cattle diseases that are of concern have to do with respiratory illness. Nature did a great job designing cattle in many ways but somewhat missed a little when it came to the respiratory tract. As a result, cattle ranchers put a lot of effort into preventing illnesses that could eventually lead to pneumonia. But even with the best of management practices, sometimes there are cattle that simply need to be treated for the disease that eventually becomes evident. This is when antibiotics come into play.

Antibiotics are a class of medicine used to treat bacterial infections. Whenever I get a group of people where we are talking about vaccines and antibiotics, I always ask, "What's the difference, and what are they effective in treating?" This, of course, is often followed by glassy-eyed stares and the occasional glance at the ceiling by those in the discussion, more evidence that maybe these pharmaceuticals should be discussed more often.

Vaccines have been developed to be able to fend off both viral and bacterial invaders. However, antibiotics are only effective against bacteria, *not* viruses. Let me repeat that: antibiotics are only effective against bacteria, *not* viruses! This may be a book about cattle production, but this tome can also serve as a public health announcement. Just because you or our animals feel sick does not mean you or our animals should be administered antibiotics. The overuse of antibiotics in human medicine, when there was only a viral infection, has led to some of the challenges we now face with antibiotic resistance in humans.

There has certainly been criticism of the overuse of antibiotics in livestock. I'm not denying those claims, but I'm also certainly not going to endorse them. The reality is that all of us need to be diligent about the tools and resources we have been given, and that includes antibiotics. But let me make a little bit of a statement. Although a large amount of antibiotics are used in animal agriculture, and a large amount of those antibiotics are used in cattle, this topic has become grossly oversimplified. It's much more complicated (like many things in the cattle world) than just quantity of antibiotics used in the cattle community.

First, let's consider the types of antibiotics used to treat infections. The veterinary and human medicine communities, whether by design or accident, actually do not cross over a lot of the antibiotics used by either area. In human medicine, penicillin is a big player, but it's actually used in rather small amounts in livestock. Tetracycline, however, is one used to treat a multitude of illnesses in animals, whereas it is rarely used in human medicine.

One of the greatest amount of antibiotics used in animal agriculture is one called ionophores. Ionophores are used to increase the amount of the more efficient bacteria in the rumen of cattle by killing off the less efficient bacteria. And by the way, ionophores are *not used at all* in human medicine. Maybe not the best analogy, but think of how probiotics might be used to encourage more beneficial bacteria in one's gut. Ionophores do something similar in that they allow for more efficient bacteria in the rumen to be prevalent by suppressing the growth of the much less efficient bacteria. If you want cattle to be more efficient, ionophores should be something you're a fan of even though they are technically antibiotics.

Secondly, cattle ranchers do the best they can to avoid having to use antibiotics at all, not only because antibiotics for treating diseases are costly to use and require high doses (because the animals are really big), but it is also often a sign that something is amiss in the health of the herd. I recall distinctly visiting with a cattle rancher in Kansas one time who was bragging about how he was so happy that he had to throw away two big bottles of antibiotics because they had expired. Some may think of this as such a waste, or how can he be happy because those antibiotics are very expensive? But from the cattle rancher's perspective, it meant that his herd was in such great health that even though he had the medicine on-hand in case one of his animals became sick, the medicine actually expired before having to be used because he never had a need to use it. That's awesome! That's the goal of those in animal agriculture, especially cattle ranchers. But the reality also is that if the animal does get sick, it's the responsibility of the cattle rancher and the right of the cattle to give that animal medicine so that it becomes well again.

The final point about the complexity of antibiotic use in the cattle community is one that I've already made mention of, which is that cattle are big. Before being administered an antibiotic, cattle will be weighed, or their weight will at least be estimated, and they will be given the correct dose of the antibiotic to help make them better. Think of the last time you went to the doctor and the amount of antibiotics you were given, if indeed you have ever been given antibiotics. Relatively speaking, I'd say that we humans probably receive much higher doses, pound for pound, than your average common cow. Cattle are big creatures, most often weighed in hundreds, if not thousands, of pounds. To take care of a big animal will require a big dose. That is why vaccination and good animal health management is so critical in the cattle-raising world. Cattle ranchers put a lot of effort and pride into maintaining the health and well-being of their animals, and if that means giving a bull some medicine so that they can combat an infection, then by golly, cattle ranchers will do it because they care about the life of that animal.

Weather

If you really like working outside, then maybe getting your very own cow might be a good move. However, be aware that, from my experience and from the experience of many a cattle rancher, Murphy's Law seems to be strongly in effect in the cattle business when weather is involved. If something bad is going to happen, it's often going to happen in the most inclement of weather conditions.

The majority of beef calves in this country are born in the winter and early spring. In more northern latitudes, this practice allows for cows to be grazing highly nutritious pasture while lactating and feeding that calf when it hits its growth spurt. However, in northern latitudes, this also means contending with winter weather conditions during calving season.

Let's face it, we raise most cattle outdoors, especially beef cattle. It makes sense. I keep saying it, but I'll say it again: cattle are big. This means that if we were to provide a barn for every animal, it would make your steaks cost a whole lot more, and we'd be covering up that much more land with buildings. But having cattle outside doesn't mean that they aren't happy. Quite the contrary.

For cattle, forty degrees Fahrenheit is "shorts and a T-shirt" weather for them. When the daylight starts getting shorter, cattle will grow longer hair in preparation for cooler weather. I often refer to my family's cattle in the winter as "wooly bears." They have fur-lined leather coats that can really help keep away the chill. Also, they have their rumen with all of the fermentation constantly going on. That microbial activity in their gut acts as an internal furnace and keeps them nice and toasty, even on the coldest of days. Usually, a windbreak is the most structure cattle will need to stay comfortable during the winter months. With the exception of a rare early wet snow, cattle can handle the cold weather quite well. Yet in the really cold parts of the country, there are indeed barns set aside for calving to allow for that wet newborn to get dried off before venturing out into the world with momma.

Actually, it's the hotter weather that cattle may need a little help with. Most of our beef cattle breeds in North America have their origins in Northern Europe and the British Isles—cool climates. This means that those animals do quite well in our northern latitudes but may need a little extra attention where it gets a bit hotter.

Cattle, like people, don't like to eat much when they're hot. Their rumen keeps cranking out the heat, and they just feel lazy and want to find shade. Thankfully, cattle ranchers realize this and have continued to make every effort they can to provide shade for cattle in the warmer areas of the country. We're even finding that adding shade, something as simple as some netting overhead to cut down on the direct sunlight, cattle seem to be more comfortable and, in turn, will eat more. If beef cattle are eating more, they grow more meat; if dairy cattle are eating more, they make more milk. Best of all, in any case, they're more comfortable and content. Many dairy cattle farms have large open-sided barns that allow for breezes to blow through but also provide a shade cover for cattle to hang out in. Feed yards will sometimes even turn on large sprinklers to help with evaporative cooling of the cattle on really hot days, and as a bonus, the sprinklers keep down dust as well.

Cattle looking for respite from the sun is nothing new to ranchers. If you're looking for your cattle in rangeland on a hot summer day, check the trees and brush. They're probably bedded down and waiting for the sun to set before they head out to do cattle stuff.

I've mentioned all of this because the job of raising cattle does require working in the elements. Sometimes it's hot; sometimes is cold. I'll be so bold as to say that cattle handle the weather much better than us fragile humans. Regardless, it's out we go to make sure that our animals in our care are getting just that. Many a time I've been out in blowing icy rain, making sure that my livestock are fed. More than once, I've been sweating through my shirt to make sure that the fences are mended well to keep the cattle from wandering off. My neck has taken on a rosy color, while my face and clothes take on a hue resembling that of the dirt and dust around me, while I gladly spend time caring for my cattle. It's not necessarily an easy job living and working with cattle, but it's definitely worth it (more to come on that thought).

Production practices

Cattle are magical creatures, not in the sense of, say, unicornish magical creatures, but they are amazing in that they can thrive in just about any environment. This means that they can also be raised under a multitude of management practices. Just like there are many different cars available for purchase, depending on the desires and needs of the end customer, there can be many different types of beef and milk available for folks to consume.

So far, we've mentioned the very traditional means of making meat and milk. Using the four segments of the beef industry helps with efficiencies that can be gained by specialists in those times of a beef animal's life and, therefore, better utilize resources to raise the beef and care for the animals while doing so. Many dairy farms borrow similar practices seen in the beef community to help with efficiencies and resource utilization as well. Yet there are those consumers out there who prefer to support agricultural practices that have a bit more of a story and connection to what may be perceived as more *natural* to them. Cattle ranchers have a solution for that as well!

The overwhelming majority of beef and dairy products are going to be produced in a way that provides an efficient, safe, and tasty product in the end using many modern practices that help provide for efficacious use of time, animals, and resources. This means feed yards, big tractors and equipment, and growth-promoting technologies in the beef world. But for consumers who prefer meat and dairy products raised in what might be considered a more picturesque bucolic fashion, cattle and dairy producers have begun to refocus their efforts on products that will meet that demand.

Let's focus on some of the marketing claims. The buzzwords of *organic* and *natural* have graced sections of grocery stores for quite some time now, but what do those terms really mean? From a purely scientific sense, I learned from my college science chemistry professor, anything that is organic simply means that it is made of chemicals containing carbon atoms in it. Not quite what most folks would connect with "organic food," but hey, vocabulary has a tendency to evolve over time.

What organic now means in the food sense, especially meat and milk, is that the animals from which the food is derived is raised under very strict guidelines that would be what most folks would consider as having the least amount of industrial enhancements imparted into the production of such food. To most, this means no pesticides, herbicides, or man-made fertilizers to grow crops. But in the livestock community, all that is true—and more.

Beef and dairy cows raised under an organic system must first themselves be deemed *organic*. This is a bit of a mystery to me, but my understanding is that the lineage of those animals must come from organically raised stock. That means that those animals are fed and raised on pasture and feed that do not see pesticides, herbicides, and man-made fertilizer, while the animals themselves are never administered any antibiotic or growth-promoting technology (e.g., hormone implants).

For farmland to be deemed organic is a bit of a mystery to me as well. What I've learned from USDA resources is that if land can be confirmed that no artificial chemicals have been applied to it in a continuous period of three years, then it can receive the rating of organic farm ground. There's a lot of paperwork and fees involved, but that land can ultimately begin producing organic feed for livestock. I'm not quite sure what the three years confirm. To me, it seems a bit of a random time frame, but that's the ruling, and by golly, that's what makes it *organic*.

If you've ever purchased organically grown food, you'll very often notice those items bring with them a higher price tag. I'm going to be bold here, but it's not because those items taste better or are necessarily better for you (based on science, not based on my opinion). They simply cost more to produce because of inefficiencies associated with that means of production. Great improvements in agriculture and food production have been made in the last century in an effort to produce food at a lower cost with fewer inputs while at the same time using a smaller and smaller farming and ranching population.

Current organically raised food is rather counter to these scientific innovations. The idea behind organically raised food is to focus on food production with less impact on the environment, which, in itself, is certainly a noble goal. Yet we need to look at the true impact of organic farming and ranching and find a balance to allow for food production capacity to continue to increase for humanity's sake while maintaining proper environmental stewardship. If you want to investigate this philosophy more, look into

Dr. Norman Borlaug, said to be the father of the green revolution. He may not agree with the way that organic food is being produced these days, but *that*, now, is my opinion.

A lot of misinformation about advancements in agriculture has been proliferated throughout society by folks who are very likely well-meaning but fail to see the big picture *and* who do not tend to work directly with agriculture to find a solution. Indeed, we instead see a somewhat adversarial approach to agriculture solutions (and that sort of approach rarely benefits everyone). For a very long time now, farmers and ranchers who utilize modern food-production practices in order to have a fiscally sustainable and environmentally sound operation have been accused of growing food with no regard for the environment and with the sole goal of making money. I'm sure that history has seen a handful of these characters, but those who abuse the environment do not last in the farming and ranching world. It is those who have found a good balance and respect for the land who are successful.

And furthermore, farmers and ranchers, although they can indeed make a good living, are not overflowing with financial abundancy—all of that to say that we should not shy away from modern food production technologies but rather embrace them as tools to help us continue to thrive as a society. In the case of beef cattle, that means utilizing growth-promoting technologies with the cattle to help them become more efficient and result in less uses of natural resources while still producing the same amount of beef or more. It's the acceptance of the safety and value of genetically engineered crops that use less water, fewer pesticides, and thereby less fuel burned in tractors to care for those crops that, in turn, helps us feed our human population, as well as our cattle, and produce safe, nutritious, and tasty protein, which not only nourishes but enhances the human experience.

To briefly address the thoughts on growth-promoting technologies—specifically, steroidal hormone implants in beef cattle—we must look at the history and context of the technology. Hormone implants have been safely used in beef production since the 1950s. That's a pretty good track record. They are only used in animals destined for food immediately and pretty much only used in young beef heifers and steers. The implants themselves range from the size of the metal tip of a ballpoint pen to the size of the spring used in that same ballpoint pen. Tiny amounts of estrogen or testosterone or both implanted under the skin of the ear of a beef steer will have a tiny trickle of hormone that helps to stimulate some additional growth of the beef animal over a period of several months. The use of these growth promoters can help grow an additional thirty to sixty pounds over the life of the animal.

Although that doesn't sound like much, it may be the difference between profit and loss for the rancher using that technology. It makes the animal more efficient at growing lean muscle (not fat) and helps them be more effective with the feed they eat.

There are certainly beef items out there that have the "no added hormones" or "naturally raised" claim for those consumers looking for that particular type of product. Let's be very clear here, however: this does not mean hormone-free. There's *no such thing* as hormone-free food (with the exception of salt). Hormones are naturally occurring chemical messengers in the body of animals and plants that tell the cells of the organism to do many tasks. Estrogen and testosterone in the growing body of beef animals help with their muscle growth. Does this mean that if a male human eats beef that had an estrogen implant, he will begin to exhibit female physical attributes? No. Does this mean that an adolescent female human who eats beef from an animal that was given an estrogen implant will come into puberty sooner? No. Does this mean a woman who eats beef from a steer given a testosterone implant will exhibit male physical attributes? No. Does this mean that men who eat beef from an animal given a testosterone implant will grow massive quantities of muscle? Still no.

The difference between a steak from an animal given an implant and one not given an implant is nearly undetectable. Although we now have scientific instruments precise enough that can indeed identify differences between the two products in question, the amount is so small that there's no way that it could impact the growth and development of male and female humans who consume beef, especially considering the massive quantities of estrogen and testosterone that males and females of the human species, regardless of age, naturally produce each day.

This is the precision of science and the massive nature of beef cattle. The tiny slow-release implant under the skin of the ear of beef cattle is just enough to cause a response for the animal to grow a bit bigger over the course of many months of its life. It's a decision that helps grow more meat with fewer animals, using fewer resources, allowing minimal impact on the animal, with practically indistinguishable differences in the meat in a safe, practical, tried-and-true manner.

For those who can afford meat, milk, eggs, and produce organically raised, I applaud you. But we must realize that conventionally farmed food has helped to make less of an impact on the environment in which it is raised while allowing for greater food availability to the world. We as a human society need to find the happy balance, and I wholeheartedly believe that cattle and the food cattle supply to humanity are part of that balance and a key to whole-earth sustainability.

Back to the original question: when you run out to start your herd of beef or dairy cattle, will you choose to utilize the modern scientifically sound feed resources and growth-promoting technologies, which provide for a safe and inexpensive source of meat and milk, or will you choose to take some steps back from technology and seek the clientele who have additional expendable income, who can afford the higher cost of *naturally* and *organically* raised animal proteins?

Either decision is not incorrect, just different. There are benefits and challenges to either approach, the breadth of which could not possibly be discussed in this book alone. In either case, my hope is that folks continue to simply see cattle as an amazing source of food and an incredible piece to a whole-world approach for meeting the needs of a hungry humanity.

CHAPTER 8

It's Not a Cow—It's a Way of Life

I have been blessed to have lived with cattle (and horses, and sheep, and chickens, and, and, and…) nearly my whole life. I finally came to this realization (the blessed part) when I was in college and found that growing up with and around livestock was not necessarily the case with most of the United States. In my animal science courses in college, I didn't quite understand why the instructors felt the need to teach us about how to give a shot to a sick cow, how to feed hay, and where to stand to get cattle to move in a calm and quiet manner. It was just something that I grew up with. But the reality is that more and more folks are removed from animal agriculture than ever before.

I have made it a bit of a mission in life to share the good word about animal agriculture to the world. This has allowed for me to engage with people and businesses all over. An exercise I like to do with groups of people with whom I am speaking is to have a bit of an informal survey. I ask everyone in the audience to raise their hands if their grandparents lived or worked on a farm or ranch. With many hands in the air, I say, keep your hand up if your *parents* lived or worked on a farm or ranch. Many hands begin to disappear. For the remaining folks who still have hands elevated, I ask for those who *currently* live or work on a farm or ranch to keep your hand up. At this point it's usually only a very small number of those in a room who still have their hands raised, if any at all.

This example is merely representative of the current reality of those directly involved in agriculture, and it's also a probable reason why those who work and live in the agriculture community are a proud group who also feel their livelihood is under constant threat. Fewer and fewer people know how food is raised and have the context by which it has been raised, but there is an overabundance of opinions out there by many different groups of folks on how farmers and ranchers should run their operations. A bit ironic and unbalanced, if you ask me.

Why is the farming and ranching community of people such a proud, albeit small, bunch? When I say proud, it's not in an arrogant way but rather in a culturally reflective manner. Agriculture is one of humanity's longest-standing endeavors. It's what has been considered some of the defining origins of civilization. When we as people began to grow our own food rather than having to hunt and search for it, we were able to spend less time just surviving and began to truly thrive. The fact that I can sit down in my kitchen and type on my laptop in an effort to tell this story of animal agriculture is an example of how I don't have to be out searching for my next meal; it's in my refrigerator, freezer, or pantry, and it is a result of the amazing advancements in food production that has sustained our society and allowed for us time to reflect, educate, learn, share, innovate, and express ourselves via art and intellectual means. To be able to contribute to this phenomenal feat by which we all (and I mean all of us living in industrialized countries) take for granted is extremely meaningful. It's probably why President George Washington stated, "Agriculture is the most healthful, most useful, and most noble employment of man." It's using the resources of the earth in a responsible manner to provide for society one of the most basic needs: food.

Living and working in the agriculture kinship is truly that. Those making a living in agriculture, especially animal agriculture, are a pretty small group, a family, albeit at times a bit of a dysfunctional family. We do acknowledge many similar hardships, of which some were outlined in this book, but we also share many of the rewarding results of our toil. Raising a calf from a newborn up to a milking mother in a dairy herd is *really* something to see. Being a part of feeding a weaned steer to over twice its body weight and seeing the delight in the eyes of those who appreciate a good steak are pleasing and worthwhile. For those who are parents, watching children eat and enjoy a meal is delightful and moving, no matter how many times you see them do it. Having the opportunity to watch people dine and appreciate a repast is a treat for those in the agriculture community. To know that you helped in a way to satiate the daily hunger we all experience and provide energy and nourishment to the body—well, *wow!*

At a young age, I was privy to the circle of life. I helped Dad many times harvest livestock that we raised so that we could have meat in our freezer. I helped Mom in the kitchen with that meat that we had to make some of the most delightful treats for the table. I grew up in a family that was highly influenced by our Italian culture. My immigrant ancestors sincerely appreciated good meat and milk and, either by coincidence or necessity, raised their own cattle, which became part of my heritage today. I can't thank that tradition enough for what it has done for my family and me. It has given me an appreciation and insatiable appetite for learning and living within the agriculture community.

Growing up with livestock often provided an opportunity to teach. Because we had cousins and friends who did not have cattle of their own, or they lived in a more metropolitan area and were not able to own livestock, we would regularly take those interested folks out to the barn or field so that they could see and touch the animals. Teaching someone how it was safe to let a baby calf to suck on your finger was always fun. Most folks would think that it would bite them. But cattle, young and adult, do not have incisors on their top jaw, so they really can't *bite* you. And later in life, taking tours of chefs, butchers, grocery store operators, and inquisitive consumers out to a pasture or feed yard so that they can see where their beef comes from was always an eye-opening experience to them and me.

Most people have an innate interest with animals, I'm finding. I believe it's something ingrained in our makeup or an evolutionary development that helped us, as a species, survive. I noticed how nearly all people have a desire to learn more about animals during my livestock-raising career as a 4-H member taking cattle to the county fair. For those unfamiliar with 4-H, it's an organization not too dissimilar to the Boy or Girl Scouts that teaches leadership and responsibility with a focus on agriculture. As a 4-H member, I would exhibit my cattle, sheep, and chickens at shows that were open to the public. Multitudes of people would walk through the barns and look at the animals that I and my 4-H cohorts would bring to show. As time progressed and I advanced in years beyond that of a 4-H member, I continue to try to make the connection of animals, especially livestock, to the greater populace. But I'm finding that the demand for interest is far surpassed by the ability to provide reliable information, which is a bit why this book was written in the first place.

It's very easy to type into an Internet search engine a question about animals and agriculture. And for some reason, I seem to see far more misinformation than proper, sound evidence being displayed. That's why it's so important for those who truly want to know where their food comes from and how to learn more about agriculture to reach out to those who are actually in the endeavor of raising crops and animals for food. Ask a farmer or rancher.

In the United States, there's an incredible resource called the agriculture extension service (more information on this is also available on the Internet). Nearly every county in the country has these resources at their fingertips, and they're all tied to land-grant universities throughout the United States. The extension system is an immense wealth of people and information, mostly tied directly to agriculture and food production, that are available for all to utilize. This is probably one of the first places where people should go to in order to legitimately learn more about agriculture and, if the interest is there, to connect with farmers and ranchers in their community.

I know the interest to learn more about farms and ranches by visiting those locations is out there. It's the reason the whole *agrotourism* movement that is popping up all over the world. People really want to learn more about farming and ranching. But going to a touristy *farm*, although accommodating, is often just a little too watered-down for what agriculture, especially animal agriculture, really is. If you really want to learn, go to a farm; get to know a farmer or rancher. Hang out with them for a day, a week; get a summer job, offer your services, or at least buy them a cup of coffee and learn firsthand what farming and ranching really are. You'll quickly see it's not the stereotypical hayseed with the pitchfork and overalls but rather a well-educated, hardworking, calloused-hands-yet-unbreak-able-spirited man or woman who truly loves what they do and put an immense amount of effort into caring for their animals and crops.

I'm now going to appeal to the farmers and ranchers who may have stumbled upon this book. Please, please, please invite members from your community out to learn from your operation. I've said it many times so far: people are removed from where their food comes from. If we don't tell our story, someone else will. Someone else has. There are countless books, movies, and Internet publications that have sensationalized and downright sullied the reputation of the hardworking and noble members of the agricultural community. You work too hard and have too much at stake to not educate the world about where their food comes from. In fact, we all have too much at stake if we don't learn more about where our food comes from. Farms and ranches are more and more under threat of land encroachment and overregulation that it is becoming harder and harder for farms and ranches to survive. That's scary. That's where food comes from, and everyone should be concerned about that. Because the story of agriculture remains to be told at the level that it needs to be shared, we have a lofty task ahead of us.

Those of us who raise livestock definitely do not do it for the money or the glory. In both cases, there's not much of either. It's because of the outright passion for the land and the animals that we do this. We love our land, we adore our cattle, and we appreciate those who purchase our meat and milk that we raise so that we can continue to live the lifestyle we have chosen. It's not luxurious or decadent, but it *is* fulfilling, and we wouldn't trade it for anything.

In the United States, it would probably surprise most folks that the average-size herd of beef cattle is forty head. That's because there are a lot of folks, like my family and I, who have cattle as more of a side business or hobby rather than a sole income. To farm or ranch full-time, it takes a lot of overhead capital. The consuming public has an expectation of safe, inexpensive food. We in the farming and ranching community believe in this expectation, but we also have a challenge with the cost of doing business.

Because of the rapid expansion of housing developments in many historically ranching and farming communities, taxes on ranches and farms in many places have raised to the point of owning the land for food production has become cost prohibitive. It almost pains me to say that out loud (or write it down). Cost prohibitive to raise food? Wow, where have our priorities ended up? Thankfully, there's still a few folks out there who love raising food animals and crops, and we'll continue to do so as long as we are able.

This does put those who do not have agricultural experience or land at a bit of a disadvantage. This means that we as a culture need to either adjust our priorities and occupations or make it so that those in the farming and ranching community are able to keep doing what they do best: raise food for the world. Keep this in mind as policy is being made and major decisions in government are being decided. If we forget where our food comes from entirely, we're going to be in dire straits.

All this, and yet we still love doing what we do: farming and ranching. We love the reward of the hard work in building a fence straight and true. We love watching the seasons and the cattle grazing on pasture. We love seeing the enjoyment of cattle as they munch on the harvested grains that they so incredibly convert into steaks and milk. We love the tie to the land. And we love raising our children in this challenging yet satisfying way of life.

Children—what a fabulous design nature came up with. As I like to say, and contrary to the perception of most first-time parents, they're inquisitive little love machines that are mostly made of rubber. The first two descriptors of that last phrase are experienced by nearly all parents of healthy kids. The "mostly made of rubber" part, well, that's a characteristic really tested on a farm or ranch.

There's no question that kids can come in contact with dangerous events and machinery on a ranch, and it's certainly our duty as parents to prevent harm from coming to our progeny, but there's also plenty of opportunity for kids to really learn and see what they are made of out in the open air of a farm.

When living with cattle especially, kids learn quickly to respect equipment, land, and livestock. They may hear a colorful and creative declaration shared by their parents to explain the magnitude of the predicament finding oneself between a newborn calf and its momma cow. They quickly learn the value of closing a gate behind them while spending the better part of what otherwise should have been a lazy Sunday morning searching for the lost steers in the neighbor's cornfield. And they learn that when we say the fence is *hot*, it doesn't mean temperaturewise but rather that a few thousand volts of electricity will quickly gain their attention if they touch it, as was intended for the bull it was keeping in. Don't worry; it may hurt a bit, but it's really not dangerous.

What children also learn while growing up with livestock is the beauty and tragedy of life and come to learn how to cope with difficult situations early on. They learn anatomy and animal behavior. They learn the importance of soil and water management, good mechanical ability, and maintaining equipment and the environment. They learn that a little (and sometimes a lot of) dirt won't hurt you, that the smell of manure is the smell of success, and most importantly, that hard work pays off more than just financially. I'm grateful to have grown up with cattle in my backyard, and I'm blessed to be able to share that experience with my children, whether they appreciate it now or later on in life.

Living the ranching life, even though it's not personally my full-time profession, is important to me and my family. It's also really important that we share this experience and the story of cattle with the world. It's my mission in life to teach the world about the good that farmers and ranchers are doing every day. People for whom cattle ranching may indeed be their primary source of income. The heritage of raising cattle and the miracle that they are, are absolutely incredible. Learn more about cattle and their people. It may help to bring perspective to the way that nature has intended for us to live and cooperate with the resources it has provided.

AFTERWORD

An Apologetic to the Animal Sciences

f you're a graduate of the animal sciences discipline or a professional who works with cattle, beef, or dairy on a daily basis, I want to be quite clear that this book was not meant as an exhaustive scientific text but rather a means of telling our story to the population of folks who do not live and work with production livestock. There's no question that the beef and dairy cattle business and the sciences involved in the cattle community are complex and highly involved. The information here was meant to be written in a way that was concise and clear (and hopefully a bit entertaining as well) to a very broad audience, not a scientific journal. However, it certainly was the intent to utilize the data-driven information gleaned from the animal sciences to tell the story of production agriculture.

Certainly, we could have expounded upon the molecular structure of glucose and the mechanisms of glycolysis during the metabolism thereof. We could have included all known breeds of cattle. However, that would cost a lot of page space and is another book in itself. We could have delved into the complexities yet simplicities of the nucleic acids and their combinations, which make up DNA and the resulting organisms, functions, proteins, actions, and the like. But we didn't. The animal science discipline is immense, I know. That's my job. I also know that to go on and on about the details of that immense subject will likely not be of immediate interest to the greater populace. However, I do hope that this sparks that interest of some to pursue more knowledge of the subjects herein.

I know that there are some experts in the field of animal science who will read this and be saying, "Well, you just opened yourself up for a monster critique." I also know that there are those on the opposite side of the spectrum, those who believe that we as humans should not consume animal products at all, who will say nearly exactly the same. For those folks on both ends of the bell curve, I recommend you get together so you can have a lengthy debate about philosophical ideologies that will convince neither. For the rest of us 99.9 percent, I hope you found this an inviting, exciting, inspiring, and lighthearted read about one of my favorite creatures: cattle.

If folks feel inclined to write or call me, please oblige yourself. Know that I am a professional academic who welcomes discourse and the sharing of ideas. I will also mention that I am a zealous animal agricultural evangelist and will stop at little to share the good word of modern, scientifically based animal agriculture.

One reading this may notice that I don't provide references or a literature-cited section to this book. Again, this wasn't meant to be a peer-reviewed examination of the literature. This was to be a casual and fun read that also was informally educational. However, if anyone would like to have scientific references about specific points made in this book, please feel free to reach out or fact-check me, and I'm certain I can provide some solid publications that will suffice. For the rest, I would hope that a PhD in animal science with a focus on production livestock, meat, and most specifically, beef, would be evidence enough of the information provided here. Oh, and by the way, it's also a story of my day-to-day life. Go, beef!

ABOUT THE AUTHOR

Phil Bass is a real-life PhD animal scientist who grew up on the rural northern coast of California in dairy, beef, and timber country. During his formative years, he worked on dairy and beef farms, milking cows, caring for livestock, and harvesting vast quantities of feed that nourished the animals.

He earned his bachelor's and master's degrees in animal science at California Polytechnic State University and his PhD in meat science from Colorado State University. Phil worked in the beef industry for several years, where he led educational programs, innovative beef carcass merchandising initiatives, and told the story of the beef community.

Phil now holds a faculty position with the University of Idaho and loves living in Northern Idaho with his family and small herd of beef cattle.